Reflections!

LOOKING IN THE MIRROR

A Success Story of a Dynamic
Businesswoman Who Overcame
Many Challenges, Obstacles
and Roadblocks

Terry Wells-Jones

DORRANCE
PUBLISHING CO
EST. 1920
PITTSBURGH, PENNSYLVANIA 15238

Dorrance Publishing Co
585 Alpha Drive
Pittsburgh, PA 15238
Visit our website at *www.dorrancebookstore.com*

ISBN: 978-1-6393-7452-6
eISBN: 978-1-6393-7485-4

Reflections!

LOOKING IN THE MIRROR

To: Janet,

"The path to happiness
begins and ends in
the mind."

◇

Dedication

This book is dedicated to all the people that never let the size of their town determine the size of their dreams. And to all the women who dared to step out of their comfort zones and use their God-given talents and abilities to live a life filled with incredible peaks, and impossible obstacles by learning to navigate with the ability to withstand hardship and adversity by thinking and understanding quickly.

◇

Acknowledgments

I am grateful and thankful for my parents for always encouraging me to strive to be the best and for constantly reminding me that there is no such word as "can't," because the future belongs to those who believe in the beauty of their dreams, and that kind of beauty should come from within: Faith...Hope...Strength...Courage... and Dignity. I love you so much and I am proud to be your daughter.

I would like to thank my friend Betty for all of her support, encouragement, patience, and unwavering faith she had in me, while helping to put the final touches on my memoir, and for that I will be eternally grateful.

Most of all, I would like to acknowledge my husband, children and grandchildren who provided both encouragement and feedback, and who shared with me the hard work and pleasure of making my dream of writing a book become a reality.

Contents

Chapter One
Family Legacy

Looking in the mirror...when you look in the mirror, what do you see? You might say, or maybe you might think, "Wow, who is that little girl that I see staring back at me? Why is my reflection of someone I don't know? Does my reflection show who I am inside and outside? Or does my reflection show who I am and who I can be?" What I saw as a little girl was the reflection of a self-assured woman. One that was willing to be a risk taker in opening doors and paving the way for other women, especially Black women. I saw "hope" as the foundation for a better life. I knew that the mirror revealed who I truly was and that it was up to me to believe that I could overcome any obstacles to achieve my goals in life by just simply "Imagining Myself Successful." As I looked beyond my reflection in the mirror, I could see that my future was a reflection of what could be. You don't always have to look at reality exactly the way it is, but for what you can achieve if you do what you set out to do. As a young child, I learned to understand myself through the reflections of those around me.

Growing up in the 1950s and the 1960s, I was called a Colored person then a Negro. I was called both of these names until the late 1960s, when both names became offensive to people of color and were replaced with Black or African American. Today both of these names have become the dominant identifiers for people of color.I asked myself where do I start my life's journey? With all the challenges and fantastic roads and roadblocks that I have personally traveled, and had to overcome all these years to be able to live the amazing lifestyle that I have. Even though my life has been filled with incredible peaks, and sometimes impossible obstacles and roadblocks, I am going to start my life's journey with growing up picking cotton in the Deep South during the Jim Crow segregation period in the early 1950s... To the bright lights of New York City.

I was born in the Deep South in the 1940s in a small rural town called Cotton Plant during the Jim Crow segregation period. This small town is where my grandparents, my parents, and myself were born. My immediate family consisted of four people, my dad, mom, brother and myself.

I decided to start my life's journal by taking you back into slavery during the mid-1800s. Yes, I can actually trace my family history back (162 years) to June 10, 1860, which was the year that my great-grandfather was born into slavery in South Carolina, and this is where his parents were slaves and worked as a cook and field help on a plantation. Several of his children recall hearing him say that his maternal grandmother was brought from Africa to America on a slave ship when she was fourteen years old. In the late 1800s General William T. Sherman order reserved coastal land in Georgia and South Carolina for Black settlement, and that each family would receive forty acres, and he agreed to loan each settler an army mule. Six months after General Sherman issued the order, 40,000 former slaves lived on 400,000 acres of coastal land. Then in March Congress authorized the Freedmen's Bureau to divide the confiscated land into small plots for sale to blacks and loyal southern Whites. Less than a year later, President

Andrew Johnson intervened, and ordered that the land be confiscated and returned to its former White owners. This included most of the land that the freedmen had settled on, and in the end only 2,000 Blacks retained the land that they had won and worked after the war. The phrase "forty acres and a mule" evokes the Federal government's failure to redistribute the land after the Civil War. Some Blacks fought back.

While my great-grandfather was living on the plantation he learned to read and write, and during his lifetime, he accomplished a lot, especially after slaves were freed in the early 1860s. As a young freed slave, he migrated from South Carolina to Arkansas and became a sharecropper. Being a sharecropper means the White man owns the land and the house. The Black man does all the farming and then pays the White man rent and a percentage of the profit from the crop at the end of the farming season. This is how poor Black farmers tried to earn a living from land owned by the White man and were rarely able to work up from poverty. However, in the late 1800 my great-grandfather had saved enough money to buy some land, and over a period of years, he purchased over 250 acres. I have the original deed that shows when he purchased his first 33.34 acres of land from a White woman on December 12, 1894 for two hundred dollars cash which was a lot of money at that time, and it was rare for a Black man to actually own any land.

Arkansas is where my great-grandfather met his first wife, Mollie, and they had seven children. She was Native American and part of the Quapaw Tribe that had migrated from the Ohio Valley area to the west side of the Mississippi River and resettled in what is now the state of Arkansas. The Quapaw Tribe today is nearly extinct but was once one of the most essential tribes occupying several villages in Arkansas, mainly on the west side of the Mississippi River. Today the Quapaw Indians are federally recognized as the Quapaw Nation since being removed by the U.S. Federal government to Indian Territory. Their headquarters today is located in Ottawa County, Oklahoma where they own about 13,000 acres, a Casino Resort, and have about 4,800 tribal members. The state of Arkansas, or "south wind" got its name from the Quapaw Indian Tribe. My great-grandmother did not live to see any of her seven children reach adult age. After her death, my great-grandfather married his second wife, Texas, who died very young, and they had no children. As a result of hard work, good management, and help from his seven children, he gained the status of a progressive farmer with up to-date farm equipment, ample livestock, and poultry. He was highly respected for his honesty in dealing with workers and associates, his business logic, and caring for his family, home and the community.

In 1911, my great-grandfather took forty acres of his land, and had it surveyed and marked off into streets and lots, he had plans to build a little town. A conductor on the Cotton Belt train, that ran through the area, suggested he name the little town Fargo because (if you go far enough from any place on the globe, you will eventually come to Fargo). The little town Fargo, Arkansas was founded in 1911 by my great-grandfather who was a former slave. The Cotton Belt Railway provided freight and passenger service through Fargo until the 1970s, when the last portion of the railroad was abandoned. Black home owners bought lots and built homes on the land that he had surveyed. The first two established churches that were built in Fargo was the First Baptist church, and the Bethel Presbyterian, this small town then built a cotton gin, sawmill, and several general stores, and this predominately Black town population grew and thrived. My great-grandfather was a faithful supporter of the Fargo Agricultural School and was on the Board of Trustees when the school was built in 1919. In 1912, he met and married his third wife, a school teacher, and they had five children giving him a total of twelve children. While rearing and educating their children, my great-grandmother managed to combine two roles, homemaker and school teacher. My great-grandfather was a farmer, a bookkeeper for a cotton gin, a faithful deacon in his church, operated a grocery store, did carpentry work, and made burial caskets for the community. He passed on to his family an extraordinary family legacy. That each family member should be deep-rooted in Christ, love, and care for each other, and that each child should be trained to be honest, reliable, and live a disciplined, respectable life. He stressed the importance of education to his twelve children and made each of them commit to passing on the legacy to future generations. He knew that his children and their children's future depended on them getting an education. He believed in God, family, education and hard work. He died December 1, 1947, at age eighty-seven, but his legacy lives on in our family. My family still owns part of the land, and because the American Civil War was fought on a portion of his land it is written up in history books.

◇

Chapter Two
Growing Up in the South with Jim Crow/
You Can Do It!

My dad was the youngest of three children and was born in Cotton Plant in 1912. He served in the Navy during World War II from 1942 to 1946, and spent most of his time on a naval ship. After the war, he returned to Cotton Plant and worked as a foreman at the saw mill and raised cotton on his farm. Over the years, he shared so many great stories with us about his days in the Navy and growing up in Cotton Plant. He was my idol and he looks so good in his Navy uniform. I have a picture of him in his Navy uniform on my desk that I look at every day. He was a great dad, a great provider, he loved his family, and yes, "I was a daddy's girl." He died in 2007 at the age of ninety-four. When I think of him, I find myself singing and dancing to a song by Luther Vandross, "If I Could Dance with My Father Again." This song brings back so many great memories and good times that we spent together. He always gave us good sound advice and was continually telling us to strive to be the best at whatever we chose to be in life.

My mom was born in Cotton Plant in 1917 and died in 2009 at the age of ninety-two. She was the second oldest child born to my grandparents, and her mother was the third oldest child of my great-grandfather, she was born in 1892 and died in 1987 at the age of ninety-five. In 1938 my mother married my dad who lived on the farm next to where she lived. To this marriage union they had two children, my brother and myself. My parents had known each other for years and they both graduated from the Presbyterian Academy, which was a private school for Black students in the late 1930s. My mother was an amazingly beautiful woman. She loved her family and was very active in her church. This is where my brother and I were raised, never missing a Sunday. If you were too sick to go to church on Sundays, you didn't get to do anything else all week except go to school. She loved cooking and was a great cook, and she loved being a wife and mother. She did not like farming; therefore, she chose to work at a nearby hospital as head cook and was the first Black person to be hired in that position in the early 1950s. Later in life she worked as a teacher's aide. My mother was my hero. "I knew that she was the wind beneath my wings, and I knew that if I was falling, she would be there to teach me to fly." She was soft spoken, with a kind heart, and had a beautiful radiant smile. She was very wise and was always willing to help others. She taught my brother and me to have faith, the importance of love, and always gave us encouragement, and words of wisdom.

People often ask me how did Cotton Plant get its name? History tells us that in the 1800s, the first White man by the name of William Lynch came from Mississippi to this small farming area in Woodruff County and built a house, a store, and planted cottonseeds that he had brought from Mississippi. Because of the rich soil, the cottonseeds flourished, and the Black and White people living there started calling the area Cotton Plant. By 1852, the town's population had grown, and Mr. Lynch applied for a post office and was granted the name Cotton Plant.

Over the years Cotton Plant flourished, and more White farmers began moving there to grow cotton because the Black people, who were already living there, would do the farming, chopping, and picking cotton. The town was booming until the Civil War from 1862 to 1864, when many of the young men, Black and White, joined the Confederate Army. On July 7, 1862, 5,000 Confederate troops clashed with 20,000 Union troops marching from Batesville to action at Hills Plantation near Cotton Plant, which was one of the 384 battlefields where the Civil War was fought. This action near Cotton Plant has been called a decisive Union victory. During the war, many Black and White soldiers lost their lives and were buried in the Indian mounds behind the plantation's main house. The Federal Government later removed the bodies of the Union soldiers to a permanent burial place. After the Civil War, Cotton Plant quickly rebounded, experiencing its greatest prosperity in the 1950s producing a lot of cotton. A railroad line was built to Cotton Plant in 1881, and by 1890 they were shipping 1,500 to 2,000 tons of cottonseed, and 4,000 to 7,000 bales of cotton to other areas. By the early 1900s, there were four Cotton Gins and several large warehouses. By the early Twentieth Century, the railroad had tracks that ran from Helena, Arkansas to Cotton Plant, which coincided with the growth in the timber industry. By 1920, Cotton Plant was home to five large sawmills, seven woodworking factories, and the largest veneer plant in Arkansas. In the early 1900s, Cotton Plant was known as the cultural center of Woodruff County because it was rich in producing cotton and was one of the most historical areas because of the Civil War. White people came from all over to Cotton Plant to go to the Frances Opera House and the music clubs that were for White people only.

Cotton Plant suffered greatly during the Depression, when the price of cotton dropped five to ten cents a pound (from a high of thirty cents), which resulted in the closing of several cotton mills and two banks. Things were almost as bad as during World War II when most of the young men went off to war.

In the early 1880s, "The Presbyterian Church" Board of Missions founded the Cotton Plant Academy School, which was a private co-educational boarding school in Cotton Plant, to educate the freed slave children. This school was part of the Northern Presbyterian Church that was responsible for founding schools for Black Americans across the south after the Civil War. The Reverend Frank Potter was the principal and was assisted initially by two teachers. In 1910, Mr. Stinson became the academy's principal, which had an enrollment of over 174 Black students. The school had a thirteen-acre campus, and part of the campus was used for farming vegetables. There were dormitories for male and female out of town students. In the 1900s, a new two story-brick building just for females was built. Black students came from other cities and states to attend and get an education, where only college preparatory subjects were taught. Few public schools White or Black in Arkansas at that time provided a college preparatory curriculum. The income to run the school was provided by the boarding students and a small tuition from local day students but was primarily funded by the Presbyterian Church. The school provided an education for Black students for more than forty years. My parents came from families that believed in the importance of education; therefore, they both had an opportunity to attend and graduate from the academy in the early 1930s which was rare for Black people at that time.

During the 1950s, the schools in Cotton Plant were public and segregated. There were separate schools for Whites and Blacks. My parents chose to pay the tuition to send us to "The Presbyterian Academy" private school. We both had an opportunity to attend the academy until it closed its doors in the mid-1950s. Once it closed, we had to transfer to The Cotton Plant Vocational segregated public school. It was a major adjustment because of the number of students per classroom and the academic programs that were offered. I can remember being devastated that the academy was closing. Initially, we had a lot of challenges with some of the students who thought, that we thought, we were smarter. We encountered a few fights before settling in and feeling like we were part of the public school system. As I look back, I know that it was those years at The Presbyterian Academy that I had an opportunity to build my educational foundation, focusing on the importance of education, working hard, and striving to be the best at whatever I wanted to be. This was a family tradition that has been passed down from my great-grandfather, grandparents, and parents.

Growing up my parents did not allow us to use the word "can't". My parents believed that you could be and do anything you wanted if you believed in yourself, set goals, and strived to reach those goals. I grew up believing that the more successful I became, the more I could help others to achieve their goals as long as they kept an open mind to the possibility that they could be successful. I reinforced this belief in my children that there was no such word as "can't," and that their success in life lies in their own hands, and they were in charge of their own life. I was always stressing to them that education would offer them an opportunity to be successful. Where they could shape and control their own life, and it would be up to them to make it happen. My philosophy in life has always been to, "Shoot for the stars and if you miss, you will land on the moon."

Being very young and having gone to a private school with students from other cities and states, I guess I never realized how much racial discrimination there was in my own hometown, the Jim Crow Laws that were put in place in the late 1880s after enslavement ended to separate White people from Black people, because many White people feared the freedom that Black people had. As a results states in the south began to enforce racial discrimination by establishing different laws to separate Black people from White people. "Free but Not Equal." The most common type of Jim Crow Laws in every southern state forbid intermarriage. It stated that it was unlawful for a Black person to play with or be in the company of a White person, and that all public facilities, e.g., water fountains, toilets and transportation, like trains and buses had to have separate facilities for Whites and Blacks. All public schools were segregated, and Blacks were legally required to attend separate public schools, and churches. There were signs in all restaurants, bus and train station seating areas, restrooms, water fountains and all public places. All the signs were marked "WHITE ONLY" or "COLORED ONLY," and it was enforced by the law. All restaurants had a separate section for Black people which generally was in the back. At the movie theater all White people would sit downstairs where they had a nice seating area, the Black people had to sit upstairs in a very small, confined area. I can remember some of the Black kids throwing popcorn down on the White kids. If they got caught throwing popcorn they would be removed from the theater and sometimes punished. I remember that Saturday was the big day that all the people that lived on the farms came into town to shop and visit with family and friends. It was like a holiday every Saturday. I remember that if you met a White person on the sidewalk while shopping on the main street where all the stores were located, the Black person would have to step aside to let the White person pass. When going into a department store, Blacks were not allowed to touch or try on any clothing, and at night all the Black people would end up on the back street where there were a few Black owned restaurants, night clubs, and a funeral home that was owned by my uncle. The White people would stay on the main street. It seems like everyone knew their place and abided by the law, and very seldom was there a problem due to fear of what could happen to them. Those who did not obey the Jim Crow Laws could be beaten, jailed, or lynched, and the Ku Klux Klan was still very active.

In the south, the Jim Crow Laws were enforced until 1965, when the Civic Rights Act finally banned segregation in schools and other public places. However, it did little to remedy the problem of discrimination in voting rights until the Martin Luther King, Jr. march on Selma, Alabama in 1965. During the 1950s and 1960s, voting rights for Blacks in the south was the central focus of the Civil Rights Movement. An on August 6, 1965, President Lyndon Johnson signed the Voting Rights Act which banned the literacy test giving blacks the right to vote. As I look back as a young child growing up in the south in the early 1950s, that's the way it was, and no one was willing to challenge bigotry, and the Jim Crow Laws. It was a time in my life that I will never forget. I think we all accepted life as it was and had "Hopes and Dreams" of a better life. Everyone worked on just surviving, from day to day, and hoping that things would change. My dad would always tell me to, "Never let the things you want make you forget the things you have."

Living in the south every year there were always a lot of storms and tornadoes. I will never forget March 21, 1952 when the deadliest tornado (F-4) in the United States occurred in Woodruff County hitting the town of Cotton Plant leaving 209 people dead out of a population of 1083. It was about 5:30 p.m. My family was having dinner when all at once, it got very dark outside; there was a lot of lightning, thundering and winds up to 200 miles per hour. Being very young, I was fascinated with the storm. I jumped up and ran to the back porch just in time to see the lightning hit the big tree in the back yard and then strike the porch just above my head, setting both on fire, leaving me completely paralyzed. My dad ran to my rescue, and fortunately, I had not been struck by the lightning just frozen in place with fear. Shortly after that we heard sirens everywhere with rescue people from all surrounding areas. It had been a powerful tornado cutting a path of devastation through the town. When the tornado reached our home, we were very fortunate it lifted up off the ground and passed over our house, then dropped back down to the ground, destroying everything in its path. The storm was so powerful and had so much wind that it picked up cars and toss them through the air, wrapping them around trees, some with people still inside their vehicle. Many homes and buildings were completely destroyed, and a lot of farmers lost everything they had worked their whole lives for. In the aftermath, 209 people lost their lives, and hundreds had been injured. The reaction to the storm was swift, with the community coming together to dig out survivors from the wreckage. I will never forget that day, it was the worst day of my life. Just listening to the sound of thundering, lightning, and the wind blowing up to 200 miles per hour was frightening. There were so many dead people that were being picked up and put into the back of trucks to be taken to the morgue, and injured people put into ambulances to be taken to nearby hospitals. A lot of people that we knew lost their lives in the tornado. To this day, I am still petrified of storms and tornados, but thankful to God my family survived with no injuries or damage to our home.

As a young Black girl growing up in Cotton Plant during the 1950s, farming was the way of life, and most farms were owned by White farmers. There was a lot of cotton grown in Cotton Plant that needed to be chopped and picked in the spring and fall of each year. This is how most Black people earned money to live. In the spring of the year, Monday through Friday, trucks and wagons would pick people up early in the morning and take them to the White man's farms to chop cotton. I remember that they were paid $3.00 (which was a lot of money in the 1950s) a day to chop cotton with a hoe from sun up to sun down in severe hot and humid weather. Then in the fall of the year, it was time to pick the cotton. That's when you would put on a long white cloth sack with straps that went across the body to put the cotton in as you pick it. You could stand, or you could crawl on your knees when picking the cotton. Normally most people picked one row at a time until the sack was filled with cotton. When the sack was filled you would take it up to a wagon to be weighed on a large hanging scale, and after it was weighed, it would be dumped into the wagon. Weighing the cotton was my brother's job. Since I was very good with math, my job was bookkeeping. I would keep records of how many pounds of cotton each person picked. After my dad got off from work at the sawmill, he would come out to the farm, bring the money to pay the people, and then drive them back into town. At the end of each day, the wagon would be filled with cotton, and my dad would hook the wagon up to two mules and take it to the cotton gin in town to be processed and shipped out by railroad to other parts of the country to be used to make fabric, which was then used to make clothing, and bedding. I did not do a lot of chopping or picking cotton, because my dad owned his farm, and my brother and myself were in charge of overseeing the people picking the cotton. This allowed my dad to keep his job as a foreman at the sawmill. Each day he would pay us a small salary, and we could use the money to buy candy, ice cream, or other things that we wanted. I will always remember the day that my dad first told me that he wanted us to manage the farm so he would be able to keep his job at the sawmill. I was so afraid that we would not be able to do the job because we were very young, but my mother looked at me and said, "Don't worry. You can do it," and I believed that we could, and we did. I must have heard those words thousands of times because she always said them with total conviction. My mother's confidence in me became the theme of my childhood, and has stayed with me all of my life. "Don't worry. You can do it."

Our family situation made it necessary for me to learn to do some things that most children were not expected to do at such a young age. My brother and I truly enjoyed our jobs and felt very important to take on so much responsibility. I am sure this is where my sense of responsibility and work ethic began, and was also the beginning of the foundation for my successful business careers later in life in the corporate world, and as an entrepreneur business owner of two retail stores.

I knew at a young age that farming and living in the south was not the life that I wanted. I guess I got that from my mother. All through my childhood, my mother repeatedly told me, "Anything anyone else can do, you can do better!" After hearing that enough times, I was convinced that I could do better. Therefore, I spent as much time as possible studying in order to get straight A's, be-cause a B was not acceptable. I worked very hard because I did not want to disappoint my mother or myself. I knew there had to be other opportunities available for me somewhere outside of Cotton Plant. I dreamed of finishing high school, going away to college, and majoring in Pre-Med to become a doctor, which was a stretch, because during the 1950s and 1960s, most Blacks that went to college wanted to be school teachers. That's because most large corporations were not hiring Blacks in sales or management positions. I had always known that I did not want to be a teacher, therefore being a doctor was an attainable goal for a Black person to achieve, and it would give me a chance to help other people. My mother taught me to be a risk taker with a competitive spirit, which has kept me going through some tough times. I would often find that sometimes, I was competing with myself, but my mother would continuously encourage me to look to the future and always put my best effort into everything I did. I always envisioned that one day the doors would be open for job opportunities for Black women who were willing to pay the price and dared to dream of being successful.

June 10, 1860   Dec. 1, 1947
Greenville,   Fargo,
S.C.   Ark.

GREAT GRANDFATHER

GREAT GRANDMOTHER

GRANDFATHER

GRANDMOTHER

MY DAD

MY MOM

MY MOM, ME AND BROTHER

ME, DAD, AND BROTHER

Chapter Three
The Night from Hell

My life in Cotton Plant was going great. I was fourteen years old in the ninth grade and looking forward to high school. Then one night, after my basketball game, my whole world became an unbelievable, "nightmare from hell," and the worst day of my life. I found myself in a situation that I did not know how to handle. Usually, after a night game, I would walk home with my girlfriend, but she was ill and did not play basketball that night. On my way home, I accepted a ride with someone that I knew, and before I realized what was happening, I found myself in a situation that I did not know how to get out of even after saying NO. After struggling to free myself from this nightmare, I jumped out of the car and ran home, frightened and scared to death. My dad opened the front door and immediately knew that something was wrong by the look on my face and my clothes were in total disarray. I was crying, so my dad immediately began to question me about what had happened. My first mistake was accepting a ride home, which was against my dad's rules. After hearing what had happened to me, my dad was so angry, he got his gun, and was going out to find the person who had taken advantage of his daughter. At this point, my mom was hollering and screaming at my dad to think this through before taking any actions. I had never seen my parents so upset. My mom and dad talked about what had happened and how to best handle the situation. My dad was so upset and angry. He finally left home without the gun to find the person. Thank God, he did not find him that night because I know the outcome would not have been good. However, the next morning my dad was up early, threatening to have the person arrested. When you live in a small rural town in the south, everybody knows everybody, and my mom did not want to send someone's son to prison. Therefore, it was a challenging and difficult decision for my dad and mom to agree on how to handle it. My mom and my grandmother finally convinced my dad to just let it go. We all tried to let it go unresolved and hoped that I would not be pregnant at age fourteen. During those times for a teenager to get pregnant, it was a real disgrace for her and her family. You were labeled as being a bad person with no future. I prayed every day that I would not be pregnant. But after six weeks, I had to come face to face with the night that my life changed and had become a "Nightmare from Hell," "I wanted to die." Once we knew for sure that I was pregnant, a plan was quickly put into place for me to move to Milwaukee and stay with relatives to help avoid some of the gossip and stress that would be placed on me and my family. I did not want to leave my family and go to live with relatives in a new town, but I wasn't given a choice. Everyone thought that this would be the best thing for me to do. "No one asked me what I wanted to do." At that time, abortions were not an option, and with my mother being a very religious person she would have never approved. I cried every day before leaving for Milwaukee. It was hard to believe that I would be the only one that would have to live the rest of my life with this terrible night from hell that had become a reality. In today's world would this be called "Rape?" I don't know, but my dad was so angry with the decision that he had to make about doing nothing, that no one in my dad's house ever discussed that night again. Was this to be a family secret to be hidden in the closet and forgotten? No, because I was fourteen years old, pregnant and going to have a child.

My grandmother kept telling me to keep my head high and not let this dictate my future. She said, "You can overcome this by working hard, and putting your life right back on track only you can do this, but it will take strength, courage, willpower, and belief in yourself." She always said, "Once a lady always a lady." She kept saying that only you can determine your destiny, just know that we will always be here for you and that this is only a temporary stumbling block. I had always spent a lot of time with my grandmother, asking her many questions about our family history. She was very wise, positive, encouraging, and a great listener. She always gave great uplifting advice. She would never repeat things twice. She believed that if you were listening, it was not necessary to repeat anything. If you ever asked her to repeat something she would say, "I don't chew my cabbage twice," so I learned to be a good listener at an early age, which paid off later in life during my business career, where being a good listener became one of my strongest selling skills.

After knowing that I was pregnant, all arrangements were made, and my mother packed up my clothes, and I took the train to live with my cousin and her husband in Milwaukee. There are no words that I could express that could ever repay them. I will forever be thankful for their support at a time when it was needed. Once in Milwaukee, it took making some major adjustments, and I was truly blessed that I had a lot of family support on both ends of the country. For over a year, I was so angry and unforgiving toward the person who caused this problem. However, my mother kept telling me, that he who cannot forgive others breaks the bridge over which he must pass, for every person needs to be forgiven. I really did not understand what that meant, but I loved my mother and trusted her judgement and wisdom, and years later was able to forgive the person, and move on with my life.

As I look back many years later, I have a lot of great memories of those years growing up in Cotton Plant, going to school, playing basketball and the afternoon yard parties that my mom would let me have to invite over a few friends for roasting hot dogs, marshmallows and of course drinking red Kool-Aide. At age eight, I was taking train trips by myself every summer to visit relatives in St. Louis, Detroit, and Milwaukee. This is when I first realized that there was another world out there with more to offer than living in the south, I was always surrounded by family and love with both of my grandparents living near on a farm, and they had always stressed the importance of love and helping each family member to get an education, which was the key to opening the door for each person to move further ahead in life. I will always remember visiting with them, and the great times I had bathing in a tin tub, pumping water on an outdoor pump, the wood burning cookstove, and the outdoor toilet, which was an experience that I will never forget. My grandparents were very loving, caring and wise. I have many great memories of my Cotton Plant classmates that I shared so many good times with, and some of them I am still in touch with after all these years. My best friend that I have known since we were babies is from Cotton Plant and we are still good friends.

The few years that I did attend the Cotton Plant Vocational seg-regated public school, it was my science teacher that had the most significant impact on my life. He saw potentials in me that I did not see. He always encouraged me not to settle for being mediocre just because things came easy for me. He told me that I should always strive to be a leader.

During the early 1960s, I had an opportunity to participate in the Civil Rights Movements led by Dr. Martin Luther King, Jr. which was a struggle for social justice for African Americans to gain equal rights, and put an end to public schools and public facilities being segregated by "Race" in the south under the Jim Crow laws. The Civil Rights Act of 1964 finally banned segre-gation in schools and other public places. But it did little to remedy the problem of discrimination in voting rights, until after the Martin Luther King, Jr. march in 1965 in Selma, Alabama, and on August 6, 1965 President Lyndon Johnson signed the Voting Rights Act into law which banned the literacy test for African Americans, allowing them to vote without having to take a literacy test.

In 1968, I was not living in Cotton Plant when integration came to the public schools, and a lot of White families did not want their children to go to school with Black children, so they moved to other towns, and the population of Cotton Plant dropped drastically. By 2004, the integrated public high school closed and was consolidated with a school in another nearby town. Today Cotton Plant has no schools, industry, and only a few businesses, and the city struggles economically. Most of the downtown area has been demolished, and only a few of the fine homes owned by Whites remain. Even though the population has dwindled, Cotton Plant is still one of the most historical sections of Woodruff County. During the Labor Day weekend which is known as "Cotton Plant Day" the town is booming and filled with people from all over that once lived there and come back annually to celebrate with family and friends.

Chapter Four
A New Beginning

After my son was born, my parents decided to pack up and leave Cotton Plant. They moved to Milwaukee where I was living. They bought a home and both got jobs. My mom got a job as head cook for a private boarding school for girls, and my dad got a job working at a meatpacking plant. They decided to move to Milwaukee because they wanted to be close to help me raise my child and help me achieve my goals in life. Because I was so young, my parents decided to adopt my son. I know that without their love, help and support I would have never been able to achieve my goals in life. I loved my parents more than they could have ever known. They were my Rock and my Foundation!

With my parents' help, I was able to continue my education and started immediately back to high school in Milwaukee. I had only missed the first semester of the 10th grade. During my pregnancy, I had been studying eight to ten hours every day so I would not be behind. After starting back to school and going to classes for two weeks, one of my teachers asked me if I would take a series of academic placement tests. I agreed to take the tests, and scored exceptionally high in all categories, and was placed in the 11th grade, skipping over the 10th, I was thrilled with the results and knew that I would have to work even harder to prove that I had earned that academic achievement. The high school that I attended was predominately White. During the next two years, I studied very hard to maintain a straight "A" average, which I had earned in elementary and junior high schools. I was taught by my parents to believe that you can have anything in this world you want – if you want it badly enough and are willing to pay the price. In order to get some things, you may have to give up something. I gave up part of my high school social life to have more time to study and help take care of my son. After completing two years of high school, playing basketball, running track, and working part-time, I graduated at the top of my class "Magna Cum Laude" out of 148 students at the age of sixteen with a grade point average of 4.3, which earned me a full paid four-year academic scholarship to the University of Wisconsin where I majored in Pre-Med and Business Administration. While in college my favorite classes were science especially Anatomy. The Anatomy classes gave me an opportunity to dissect and study the human body (cadaver) which was a requirement for aspiring physicians. It was an awesome experience being able to remove organs from the human body to study... i.e., brain, heart, lungs, kidney and other body organs to determine their death. Some of the students initially could not handle their first class without getting sick or fainting. My goal was to go to Meharry Medical College in Nashville, Tennessee, and become a doctor. There were two Black medical doctors in Milwaukee that were my mentors and they were going to help finance my medical school expenses. They had both graduated from Meharry Medical College. When I graduated from high school, they gave me the *Gray's Anatomy* medical book, which at that time was used by doctors to study the human body.

The University of Wisconsin campus that I attended only had two Black students on campus. My immediate goal was to recruit more Black students. On the weekends when I went home, I would try to recruit other students if they had at least a 3.5 grade point average, and were interested in going to college. Most of them were not enrolled in college simply because they didn't have the money, and were not aware of the financial aid and scholarship programs that were available. If they had a grade point average of at least a 3.5, and were interested in going to college, I would meet with their parents and help them apply for a grant, student scholarship, or student loan. Over a period of two years, I recruited six Black students giving them an opportunity to go to college. There were days, I felt like their mother trying to keep them on track, stressing to them daily why they needed to study and not be hanging out in the student center playing cards (bid wiz). My first recruit was my roommate, and she gave me the nickname "Terrible T," because I was always trying to get them to study. Each semester, I was taking eighteen to twenty hours of classes, and they were complaining about taking fifteen hours. Those were crazy, wild and exciting years, ones that I will never forget, i.e., living in the dorm, eating in the cafeteria, partying in the student center, curfews, and having no money. However, we managed to have a lot of laughs, fun, and great times together. I have so many great memories of those days, and most of the students became lifetime friends. We have kept in touch all of these years. When we have an opportunity to get together, we spend many hours reminiscing about the good old days of college life, and all the crazy things we did during those years, and believe me, we did have some "Good Old Days."

My parents taught my brother and me the importance of getting an education and helping others. Therefore, I grew up believing that the more successful I became, the more I could help others to achieve their goals in life. I would often tell my college friends that I recruited that getting an education would allow them to be able to shape and control their own life as long as they believed in themselves, and always stressing to them that their success was in their own hands, and they were in charge of their own destiny, and it would be up to them to create the kind of lifestyle that they wanted to live. I am very proud of each of them, because they listen and they have all had successful business careers. While in college, I had an opportunity to pledge Alpha Kappa Alpha (AKA) Sorority, which was the first historical African American Greek lettered sorority that was founded January 15, 1908, 113 years ago at Howard University, in Washington, D.C. AKA's goal is to focus on the depth of commitment, vision and confidence of its members. We are so proud to have one of our sorority sisters, Kamala Harris as the first woman of any color to be Vice President of the United States of America. "You Go Girl."

◇

Chapter Five
Spectacular Events/Life as a Black Model

During my third year in college, I was home for the weekend and was downtown in Milwaukee shopping when I was literally stopped on the street by the editor of the *Milwaukee Sentinel/Journal* newspaper. "She asked if I was a model or had I ever thought of being a model." I told her that I was a student at the University of Wisconsin, majoring in Pre-Med and Business Administration. She asked me if I would come in for some photo test shots the next time that I was home from school. A few weeks later, I called and set up an appointment. In my very first photoshoot, I wore a pink designer dress, which landed me a full front-page ad in color in the Women's Section of the Sunday *Milwaukee Sentinel/Journal* newspaper. This was the first time the newspaper had featured a Black (Negro) model and had never featured a model of any color on a full front-page ad. This may not seem newsworthy today, but in the mid-1960s it was groundbreaking because at that time, we were still called Negroes, and very few Black models were being used in fashion shows, TV commercials or magazine ads. The *Milwaukee Sentinel/ Journal* newspaper was sold all over the United States and other countries, and as a result of that one photo, the newspaper received a lot of phone calls from Chicago, Philadelphia, Montreal, Canada, and New York wanting to know where they could book the Creole or French model for fashion shows and ads for their businesses. I got a lot of modeling jobs from major department stores, breweries, banks, supermarkets, Pepsi, and General Motors to do print ads or TV commercials. If you look through my modeling portfolios, you will see many advertisements that ran in newspapers, magazines, banks and department stores. Stating that this was the first time they had used a Negro model. In the 1960s, it was tough for Blacks to break into the modeling Industry. I managed to get a lot of modeling jobs because of my fair complexion. My agency often booked me as a Creole or French model. My goal as a young Black model was to be successful despite the color barrier, and be a trailblazer, opening doors for other Black models. The most exciting thing that happen was when I received a telegram from Oscar de la Renta, a top Women's Fashion Designer in New York City, stating that he was interested in meeting and booking me to model his fashion designs in New York City.

After college, I shelved my medical career and situated myself permanently in New York City, where I model for Oscar de la Renta and most of the top women fashion designers, and was featured in many newspapers, and magazines, i.e., *New York Times*, *Milwaukee Journal*, *Ebony Magazine*, and *Life Magazine* modeling fashions from swim suits to full-length mink coats. I have three large portfolios crammed with photos. Some were taken in the homes of Oscar de la Renta, Amy Vanderbilt and other celebrities in New York City where I modeled for many years, and was one of the first Black women to break the color barrier in the field of fashion modeling and doing television commercials in the 1960s. In order to have a speaking part in a television commercial or motion picture, I had to be a member of an organization called SAG-AFTRA which represents performers and media professionals.

During my modeling career, I did a lot of television

commercials for Roundy's Foods out of Chicago, Pepsi, Schlitz Brewery, Miller Brewery, General Motors, and banks, and I did print ads and television commercials for banks in Milwaukee. This was their way of trying to develop a relationship between the bank and the Negro community. My agency received a lot of calls for modeling jobs from all over the United States which kept me booked especially for fashion shows with all the major department stores, i.e., Bloomingdale's, Saks Fifth Avenue, Bergdorf Goodman, Neiman Marcus, Lord & Taylor, Marshfield's, and Macy's.

As much as I enjoyed during photography, my favorite was doing runway fashion shows in New York, Philadelphia, Chicago, Milwaukee, Miami, Paris, France and Montreal, Canada. I was usually booked as a high fashion model, modeling fashions for all the top fashion designers globally, i.e., Oscar de la Renta, Bill Blass, Christian Dior and Givenchy. Nothing was more exciting than walking the runway. I had my own walk, and pivot with double and triple spins, and a special runway walk just to show off pants which were becoming popular for women in the work-place. Being five-foot-nine with long legs, I got a lot of bookings from top designers like Bill Blass, who was just beginning to show pants for women, to the buyers from all the department stores around the country. One thing I could do was walk those pants on the runaway. Usually, when I was modeling, I was told not to smile because I have dimples, and they thought my dimples would be distracting to the buyers who would focus on my face instead of what I was wearing. As a model, you are basically seen as a hanger, or just a pair of shoulders for clothes to hang on. Those years of modeling were exciting, fast pace, rewarding, and a lot of hard work. Everyone thinks modeling is all glamourous, and it is, but to be successful in this industry, it requires being able to handle a lot of rejections that sometimes hurt, but it does not have to hold you back. To be successful in the modeling industry, you must have a tremendous amount of self-discipline, and self-control to make yourself work hard without needing anyone to tell you what to do. Being successful in this industry is no accident, and there are no secrets other than hard work.

People often asked me, did I have a chance to "crossover" to acting. "Oh Yes." I was in a few movies with Sidney Poitier called *The Lost Man* (1969) and *The Landlord* both filmed in Philadelphia. Wow, it was exciting meeting and working with Sidney Poitier, Al Freeman Jr., Pearl Bailey and Diana Sands each day on the set. Those were glamourous, wild exciting times, and "YES" I did all the high-profile party stuff with all the celebrities from Studio 54 in New York City, to Martha's Vineyard, which is an island in Massachusetts south of Cape Cod that has beautiful sandy beaches, and is known for being an affluent summer colony, and is accessible only by boat or air, from New York City, and it is located on eastern Long Island. It is a summer destination where affluent New York City residents go to spend time on the beautiful beaches and enjoy all the high-end restaurants, bars and designer boutiques. I would often fly there for the weekend by helicopter from New York City. Yes, this was life in the fast lane, but I managed to keep myself grounded and not go overboard while partying with what was known as the affluent "Beautiful People" in New York City.

Life as a model was stimulating, exciting and financially rewarding, and especially to be launched as one of the first Black models in the industry. I had an opportunity to be a trailblazer, helping to pave the way, and open doors for other Black models. Over the years, I had a very successful modeling career and made $75 to $125 per hour for doing fashion shows, and a lot more for photographer shootings, TV commercials and movies. I was featured in one newspaper with my photo, and the headline read, "Model Worth a Million" making over $2,400 a week. Yes, I made a lot of money back in the late 1960s and 70s. I worked very hard because I knew that a modeling career was short-lived based on age. It was an exciting time in my life to be recognized and stopped on the streets in New York City, and to have an opportunity to meet and party with what was known as the "Beautiful People," i.e., people like Paul Newman, and his wife Joanne Woodward, and I was dating a very well-known New York Knicks basketball player that I would like to thank him for his part in my journey, and know that I will forever be thankful for the love, joy and happiness he added to our lives. Yes, the life of being a fashion model was exciting, especially for a small-town country Black girl from Cotton Plant.

Over the years people have often asked me if I ever had any regrets that I gave up becoming a doctor? The answer is NO. I always knew that I didn't want to be a school teacher, and at that time being a doctor was an attainable goal for a Black person, and being a doctor would give me an opportunity to help other people.

BEGINNING OF MODELING CAREER...PINK DRESS FULL FRONT PAGE COLOR AD IN THE MILWAUKEE JOURNAL/SENTINEL SUNDAY'S WOMEN SECTION.

PICTURE AT OSCAR DE LA RENTA HOME

PICTURE AT OSCAR DE LA RENTA OSCAR DE LA RENTA DRESS CUT UP FRONT

OSCAR DE LA RENTA SUIT AND DEER

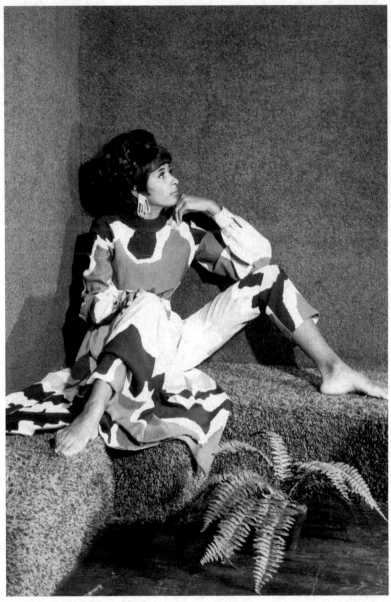

CARPET...OSCAR DE LA RENTA

CHRISTMAS EVE

AT AMY VANDERBILT BACK YARD

WHITE JUMPSUIT

GREEN JUMPSUIT

BLACK PANTS LOOKING IN MIRROR

BLACK & WHITE DRESS IN FRONT OF STEPS

LONG WHITE SKIRT

OSCAR DE LA RENTA IN FRONT OF BOOKCASE

LONG WHITE JUMPSUIT ON BENCH

COAT OVER PANTSUIT...DONALD BROOKS...UPPER EASTSIDE NYC

FEATURING SOCKS AND SUIT

OUT IN HAYFIELD

IN BARN WITH HAY

"INNOCENT LOOK"

"SEXY LOOK"

$2400 A WEEK FOR TERRY

"MODEL WORTH A MILLION"

BOSTON STORE

PEPSI TV COMMERCIAL

ROUNDY'S FOOD TV COMMERCIAL

Chapter Six
Life Changes/God Created Woman

After years of modeling, and life changes that left me a divorced single mother of two, I knew that modeling was not a lifetime career. Therefore, I decided it was time to look into a business career, utilizing my business administration degree. I am a very highly competitive person that needs to see results based on my own performance. I began deliberating and researching the job market and decided that the best way to achieve my business career goals was to become a sales representative/sales manager with a Fortune 500 company. I wanted to pursue a career that was not a nine-to-five office job. I wanted to be outside, moving around, and not sitting behind a desk. After looking through the *New York Times* Employment Section of the newspaper, I quickly realized that large corporations were not hiring women for sales positions. Then one day, while I was looking through the newspaper, I saw under the male's classified section that Beech-Nut Corporation (Gum and Life Savers Division) was looking to hire a male sales representative. I mailed in my resume and received a call from the Regional Sales Manager, who told me that they were not hiring women for outside sales positions. After speaking with him, I convinced him to invite me in for an interview. A week later, I met with him and the National Sales Manager. A few days later, I received a call from them, offering me a sales position. I would be the first female to be hired as a Sales Account Manager for Squire Beech-Nut Corporation. There was one little problem, the position was in Boston, which would require me to relocate. After giving it some thought, and negotiating my salary, company car, relocation package, and other fringe benefits, I decided to accept the position in order to get some outside sales experience. I packed up and relocated to Boston with my two children.

After the initial sales training, I was assigned a district in a suburban area of Boston where I would be marketing Beech-Nut Gum and Life-Savers to super markets and other retail stores. The district was dominated by the Wrigley Gum Corporation who at that time was the number one chewing gum company in the country. I quickly realized that I had my work cut out for me if I was going to get my products into the stores, and fight for shelf space. I would need to develop a plan and strategy to insure getting my products in the market, and to remove Wrigley Gum from the number one sales position. My plan was to develop a business relationship with the store owners and managers by showing them how much I could help them increase their sales without any extra work from them. The second thing I needed to do was to get my products on the top shelves of the display racks which were located near the check-out registers, and provide regular follow up service to ensure the availability of products. I began by providing them with new Beech-Nut display racks, and ordering the products that were needed for display. I initially set up and displayed the new racks with all the products on the top shelves, moving Wrigley Gum to the lower shelves, and I made sure that I serviced all my accounts on a regular basis. After six months, I had moved the Beech-Nut products to the number one sales position beating out Wrigley Gum. This new sales approach increased the sales in my stores, and helped me to open up a lot of new accounts. After seven months of working in the district, I was approached and offered a sales position with Wrigley Gum.

In my first year Beech-Nut had an 11 percent sales increase. My district sales made a significant contribution to the company's overall sales increase. In the company's 1973 Annual Report, they featured a picture of me on the cover, and a picture inside the Annual Report where I stated, "I know that sales is a field that women can handle successfully." I was accepted by all the accounts that I called on in my district, and was hoping to eventually get into sales management. After two very successful rewarding years with the company, I realized how much I missed my friends and living in New York City. I decided it was time to revamp my sales career objectives and focus on an industry that I loved and knew a lot about and one where I could live and work in New York City. I wanted a career where I could earn the kind of money that I had become accustomed to earning which was $75,000 to $150,000 a year with lucrative stock options, and other executive benefits. This was an extremely high salary in the 1970s, and the only business background that I had was in sales with Beech-Nut, and fashion modeling. However, as a result of my modeling career, the one thing that I knew was the fashion industry and how it worked, and these were the businesses that purchased their fabrics from Burlington Industries to make clothing for the retail stores.

◇

Chapter Seven
Fighting It Out in the Corporate Jungle

After extensive research, I decided to initiate my sales career plan and seek a sales position with Burlington Industries, which was a Fortune 500 company, and their headquarters was located in New York City. Burlington Industries was a $4 billion textile conglomerate, the largest textile company in the world, and the most diversified manufacturer of textile, and related product for the apparel market and the home. Burlington made most of the fabrics that were sold to menswear and women's wear manufacturers that made the clothes that we wear. They also made hosiery, draperies, bedspreads, sheets, towels and carpet, and operated 108 plants in ten states and twenty-two plants in nine countries, and most of their factories were located in South and North Carolina. Worldwide they employed over 75,000 people. However, pursuing a sales position in the early 1970s presented a significant challenge because there were "No Women" in a sales position in the textile industry in the entire country. I decided to take on the challenge of pursuing a sales career with Burlington Industries by breaking through the glass ceiling and becoming the first woman to be hired in a sales position. I knew that if I wanted to be that woman, I would need to be incredibly strong, unafraid of loneliness and rejection, because I would definitely face both often. In order for me to succeed, be successful and avoid being evaporated into the corporate atmosphere, I would have to learn to battle a male chauvinistic society that would seemingly be against me in order to compete. I would need to have the self-confidence of seeing myself as intellectually equal, and believe that I could compete with men. I honestly thought that once I felt myself intellectually equal, I would have a chance to be treated equally by accepting nothing less than totally equal treatment.

I knew that having a career in business would require me to be competitive, and have an achievement-oriented personality. I would need to work harder and longer in order to be emotionally challenging, and be willing to make sacrifices. I knew that if given a chance, I could and would be successful because I believed in myself, and that is where it all begins. I believed that I could over-come any obstacles to achieve my goals in life just by "Imagining myself successful."

My next step was to get an interview with Burlington Industries for their next sales training seminar. I began looking in the Sunday's *New York Times* newspaper classified employment section. At that time, the employment section was broken into jobs for men and women. I quickly noticed that all the jobs for men paid a lot more money, and that most of the jobs for women were for secretaries, nurses, and school teachers. I disregarded those job categories and mailed my resume directly to the Personnel Department manager for their upcoming sales training seminar. After one week, I received a call from the Personnel Manager. She asked to speak to mister, my first name is a unisex name, and all the activities on my resume, like my major in college being Pre-Med and Business Administration, field track, and basketball, led her to believe that I was a man. After she realized that I was a woman, she proceeded to tell me that they had "no women" in sales, and had no intention of hiring any. I shared with her my beliefs as to why they should hire a woman. I told her that women have as much innate sales ability as men and I believed that women could actually surpass men in their sensitivity to a customer's needs, and their instinct for the customer's mood and willingness to buy. I told her I knew that I could be successful in a sales position with the company if given a chance. After talking with her on the phone, she finally said that she was so impressed with my background, career aspirations and goals that she would like to set up an appointment to meet with me at her office. A week later, I met with her for my first interview. After the initial interview, she was impressed with my goals and career objectives of being a Sales Executive in an all "man's world." She immediately set up another interview for me to meet with some of the sales management team. I was excited, and could hear my dad telling me that the key to being successful in any business is to "learn the game, then play the game."

In my second interview, I spent the entire day interviewing with all the department managers up to the Vice President of Sales. After the interviews, she said they would get back to me in a few days. The next day, I received a call from her to set up an appointment for some additional interviews. At the end of the third day of interviewing, they offered me a position as the "First Women Sales Executive" in the world's entire textile industry. I was thrilled. I knew that selling was supposed to be a man's world, but I wanted to prove what I really believed. That a woman, given a chance, can sell. Because no matter what job you're in, you're always either selling yourself, or your products, and, I probably wanted the job even more because they didn't want to hire a woman. I relished the thought of being the first woman of any color to be hired in an all- Man's World, and being able to break through the "Glass Ceiling." I felt like I would not just be working to build my career, but to open doors for other women to enter into a sales career that would be challenging, and highly rewarding. I was not a strong women libber, but I did believe in equal pay for equal work. Therefore, I ensured that my salary was within the same range as the other male sales trainees. Burlington Industries was a large diversified company that was divided into many different divisions. They offered me a sales position with the Klopman Mills Division, which had two separate departments, Womenswear and Menswear. Neither department had a woman sales executive. They gave me a choice to choose which department, I would like to work for. After negotiating my salary, relocation package, and other fringe benefits, I chose the Menswear Department. I thought if I am going to be a trailblazer and the first woman hired in the textile industry, why not double the excitement, and be the first woman hired as a Sales Executive, and the first woman to sell fabrics to menswear accounts. Once again, I packed up and relocated back to New York City with my children. After being hired by Burlington Industries, all the newspapers in New York City ran articles announcing that Burlington Industries hires "First Woman Sales Executive." I received many calls from all areas of the fashion industry congratulating and wishing me loads of success.

My first week on the job was spent in the sales training seminar. Initially, my co-trainees were not very happy competing with a woman, nor was management enthusiastic. They kind of gave me the cold shoulder and tried to discourage me by telling me how hard the sales job was and how heavy the sample bag was to carry around all day. The one thing they all agreed on was that women should be in some areas of sales, but not with us. On the last day of the seminar, I asked the instructor if I could speak to the group, he said yes. I got up and said, "I know everyone is concerned about using profanity in my presence, but I want you all to know that I am 3 X 7 plus, and when I hear profanity that I have not heard, I will let you know. I am here to be part of the team, because it takes a team working together to get the job done. I don't expect to be treated any different than the other guys on the team." They all stood up and started clapping their hands, which broke the ice. It was the beginning of making me feel more like one of the guys. I could hear my dad telling me to be successful in the corporate world is to "learn the rules of the game, then play the game." As a saleswoman, I wanted to be treated as a business person, not as a woman. I wanted to make it clear that I did not want or expect special consideration. The sales team at that time consisted primarily of Jewish men. I owe a large part of the success that I had at Burlington Industries to the sales training program and the sales team. They taught me how to make an excellent presentation, and how to close a sale. I was a good listener (a skill that I had learned from my grandmother), knowing how to listen when someone talks, and pick up every nuance of the conversation. I had learned when to take the gentle approach during a presentation and when to assume a challenging sales approach.

I asked myself, what personal characteristics should a successful saleswoman have? I decided that the number one characteristic should be personality. Appearance should run a close second because when a person first meets you, they don't know what abilities you have, so personality and appearance will help get you through the door. Being a woman sometimes had a distinct advantage especially in the textile sales industry. It stimulated curiosity and interest, especially when I would hear comments like a woman selling piece goods, "Never." I always took the business approach and handled myself professionally. I did not put up with professional flirtation. "I told myself from the beginning that I was in this business to sell piece goods, not to be wined and dined." The fashion market first appears to be very large, but it is actually very small. Your reputation is established very quickly, and it must be a good one. Even on small, seemingly insignificant matters, it was essential to preserve a businesslike approach. For example, when taking a buyer for lunch, male or female, it is customary for the salesperson to pay the bill, or when going to lunch with a sales person in the same company, it should strictly be "Dutch Treat." It was essential for me not to allow my fellow salesmen to take on a superior, condescending attitude. I wanted to be treated at all times as a full-fledged member of the team.

These were some of the things that I had to learn on my own because there were no women mentors in sales at that time. Today's newspapers and magazines devote considerable space to such topics as "Opportunities for Women in Management, and Women Achievers," that have reached the Executive Suite. However, over fifty years ago, that wasn't the case. There weren't enough women to qualify for inclusive news articles, with a few exceptions of women who were trailblazers in the sales field of "All Men."

Initially, there were a few rough spots working with some of the sales guys on sales calls. Some of their major accounts patronized me as being the salesman's assistant helping him with his routine calls. Once they were told that I was the new sales executive their whole attitude changed. When the sales training was completed, I got my first list of over 100 accounts which was made up of the top high-priced designer menswear manufacturers, the toughest accounts on the streets, i.e., Bill Blass, Oleg Cassini, and Christian Dior. It was a list of accounts that no one at Burlington Industries had ever been able to sell. I asked myself, "Was this the catch? Had I been hired to fail?" Or was the thinking at that time, "Well, we hired a woman in sales, and it didn't work out."

After realizing what was happening, I decided that I was going to overcome this obstacle and roadblock by learning how to navigate through this maze with creativity, endurance, and agility. I needed to think quickly about how to solve this problem. I could hear my dad saying what you need to do is, "to learn the game, then play the game." After a few weeks of thinking it through, I saw an opportunity to build a new market for the company, by developing a foothold in the higher-priced menswear trade. I began to work on my plan of action to present to senior management. The first thing I needed to do was to hit the streets, meet my new accounts, and learn about their business, fashion lines, and their plans to increase their menswear annual apparel sales. I asked each of them if they would buy their fabrics from

Burlington Industries if I could create a new department, design a separate line of fabrics, colors, and patterns that was exclusively for the high-end menswear trade, and offer them six months to a year lead time, with co-op advertising in the *New York Times* newspaper with major department stores like Bloomingdale and Saks Fifth Avenue. They were very open to this new idea and said they would consider this new sales approach; however, no one really believed that I could get Burlington Industries to agree to this proposal, because it would cost the company thousands of dollars.

It took me a few months to get all the information together that I needed. My next goal was to put together a presentation and set up an appointment to present this new innovative sales and marketing concept to senior management. It would show them how we could capitalize on the designer menswear manufacturers. I worked day and night, gathering all the information needed to create a new color line, new fabrics, patterns and designs. At that time, Paris, France, was the world's fashion leader with new fashion concepts, working about two years ahead of the United States. I focused on purchasing men's silk shirts, neckties, and silk yarns to develop a new "color line" that would appeal to the designer menswear accounts. I would also present why it was essential to create a new department exclusively for the designer menswear trade, and name the new department "Gotham Place," which was a name that I created. I felt the name had an old traditional classy sound, and was definitely unique. This new department would give the designer menswear accounts a twelve-month lead time on colors and fabrics that they would purchase from Burlington. Then we would open the market and sell these colors and fabrics to the lower-priced menswear accounts like Sears, JC Penny's, Van Heusen, and Arrow Shirts.

The big day finally arrived for my presentation to senior management. After making the presentation and answering many questions, all of the senior executives including the president were excited about the new innovated marketing concept, and immediately decided to have this new program ready to be introduced to the menswear designer accounts for their 1976 Fall product line. I was overly excited about the opportunity to launch this new program.

After launching the program, I quickly became popular with the menswear designer accounts and began bringing in one new account after another. At the end of the first year, sales had grown from $0 sales volume to over $1.9 million, and I was promoted to the first woman Assistant Sales Manager in the textile industry. I was given my own department, which I named Gotham Place.

By the end of the third year, sales in Gotham Place had grown to over $6 million. At this point, the company decided that the department needed to have a sales manager. But were they ready to promote a woman to head up a department with that much sales and responsibilities? The answer was "NO," even though I had created and developed the department. They tried to justify why they felt that I was not ready to handle that much responsibility. They finally hired a man from outside the company that had very little knowledge of the textile industry. When I did not get the promotion that I knew I should have gotten, I was going to quit, but I decided to ride it out for at least another year, I continued to work hard, bringing in one designer account after another, and creating many new products that made me become well-known in the fashion world for men and women.

After less than one year, the new manager they brought in was let go... so now what? The talk in the industry was would Burlington Industries step up and promote me to the Gotham Place Department Sales Manager position, which I founded. After three weeks of interviewing other people from outside the company, they finally decided to promote me to the first woman in an Executive Sales Manager position to head up the Gotham Place Department. With this promotion came a big increase in salary and other fringe benefits. The promotion was the talk of the fashion industry in New York City, and throughout the country. It was written up in all the trade papers, and the *New York Times* newspaper. People in the industry knew that I was qualified but was the textile industry ready to put a woman in such a powerful position, especially a Black woman that had broken through the glass ceiling?

The Sales Manager position allowed me to be able to develop new colors, fabrics and designs for the Spring and Fall menswear fashion line. It was inspiring to be a leader in making major fashion decisions for the entire textile industry. Twice a year for Spring and Fall, my department (Gotham Place) would put together a color line, new patterns and fabrics to present to the menswear fashion industry. If I said that "Blue" would be the latest color trend for the Spring or Fall season, the rest of the fashion world from New York City to Paris, France, would begin to focus on that color as their primary fashion color for that season. It was like the old E.F. Hutton television commercial, "When E.F Hutton speaks, everybody listens." The fashion world would say, if the manager of Gotham Place predicted a specific color for the Spring or Fall season, everybody in the menswear industry was listening, and that would be the primary color promoted at the retail level for that season. I made many trips to North and South Carolina on the company's private jet to work with the factories in the development of new colors and fabrics.

After a few years with my sales team of six men and one woman, and an outstanding administrative assistant that was my right arm in every endeavor, the Gotham Place department sales had grown from zero sales volume to over $20.5 million. In 1976, Burlington Industries had the highest profit gain in sales in its fifty-three years. The increase in apparel products occurred primarily because of the company's new innovative sales and marketing concepts. Which made them be able to capitalize on the latest products developed in 1975, and presented to the fashion industry in 1976. Sales in apparel products increased in 1976 by 17 percent over the previous year. This was the year when the new designer menswear line was first introduced. I was given special recognition and featured on the cover of "Burlington 1976 Annual Report," as one of the people who developed new products by using new innovative marketing techniques to merchandise those products. There was a great write up and picture inside showing me working in the showroom with one of my major accounts. This new innovative marketing helped the company attain its goal by opening up a whole new market segment, the designer high-end menswear manufacturers. They used my own words in the "1976 Annual Report," to describe Burlington Industries. The caption under my photo on the front cover states, "I'm a woman, and I've proven that I can sell fabrics."

There are many fringe benefits in being an executive and heading up a department especially when you have an unlimited company entertainment budget. I found that the higher you climb into the executive life, the more your business is conducted in luxury restaurants over lunch or dinner with your company picking up the check, especially if you are in an executive sales management position. Part of my job was to entertain customers by taking them to plays, sporting events, country clubs, and weekend resorts, all on the company expense. All of this sounds glamorous, and it can be, but sometime for an executive businesswoman it can be a nightmare, especially if there is drinking. I would always avoid drinking unless I was totally confident that the person respected the business nature of our relationship. I always handle too friendly businessmen by a quick reference to my penchant which was to "keeping business and social lives separate." Business dinner often kept me working late, limiting the amount of time I had to spend with my children. However, it seemed to have fostered a healthier relationship with three individual lives contributing to the whole. I believed that, "It's not the quantity of time you spend with your children that counts, it's the quality of time." I found that I was able to cram into a weekend as much time with my children as most mothers fit into a full week. When I was with my children there was nothing else in my life. Evenings and weekends were strictly "family times." I had to decide whether to sacrifice my work or my social life. Since my career was very important to me, I decided to take the time from my social and leisure activities. My career success more than provided for my two children financially, and I was able to get them into the best private schools. They loved that sometimes they were able to go with me to some of my business dinners and sporting events with my accounts, and I often brought them to my office to sit in on presentations that I made so they could learn about the corporate world. This exposure apparently influenced them because they both graduated from college, and have careers in sales and marketing, and have been very successful.

I often traveled out of town on business trips with a group of male coworkers, and I didn't want to appear conspicuous as the only woman, so a tailored business pantsuit was the answer. Usually, they were made out of the fabric that I sold and were made exclusively for me by one of my designer accounts. Wearing a pantsuit was not to assume masculinity but, "I liked the way they looked." They gave me a professional look, and they affected attitude. The more business like I appeared, the more I was accepted.

◇

Chapter Eight
Applause, Applause

In 1979, I was featured in a training book published by Fairchild Publication. The book is about three of "The Most Powerful Women" in sales management positions in the textile and apparel industry. I was the only woman of the three women that was in the textile industry, and the author stated in the book, that at the time of writing, "I was known as the most successful sales talent male or female in the textile industry." The title of the book is *Woman Power in Textile and Apparel Sales*. For many years, this book was used by large corporations as a training manual as they began to hire women in sales positions. I had an opportunity to be a guest speaker at many of these corporate training seminars for women across the country. The training book focused on how to break into the world of sales, writing resumes, making presentations, closing sales, and tips on dressing. It also features a profile on each of the three women, about the challenges that we each faced and overcame to be the first woman in our fields. The author of the book interviewed Burlington Industries' Human Resource Director regarding why I was hired as the first woman in the textiles industries. He said, "If a person has the right abilities and characteristics, they can get a job in this industry." He noted that among the qualities that Burlington Industries looks for in job applicants is that high priority be given to the requirement of the job, a willingness to service the accounts, and that initiative and drive are "essentials to being successful." He also stated that calling directly on the prospective employer exhibits aggressiveness and motivation, both of which are characteristics of a good salesperson. The book is well worth reading even today for women interested in a sales or marketing position and is still available on Amazon.

During my years at Burlington Industries, I earned executive admiration throughout the $4 billion conglomerate, the largest textile company in the world. As a woman, I was determined to be successful and to break down barriers for other women. I attributed my success at Burlington Industries to what I call the three C's: Confidence, Consistency, and Courage, and a lot of hard work.

I received many inspiring achievement honors while working at Burlington Industries, which was limited to females who exhibited leadership and success in their industry.

Over the years, many articles were written about my sales career and success as the first woman sales representative, and sales manager in the textile industry. Listed below are some of the special recognitions that I received while working at Burlington Industries:

• Burlington Industries 1976 Annual Report – Featured with photo and quote on cover, "I'm a woman and I've proven that I can sell." There was a write up inside the annual report regarding my sales management achievements.

• *Woman Power in Textiles and Apparel Sales*. A training book published in 1979 by Fairchild Publication about "Three of the Most Powerful Women in Sales." At the time of writing, the author states that, "I was known as the most successful sales talent male or female in the textile industry." This book is still available on Amazon.

• The Marquis "Who's Who of American Women." I was listed four consecutive years as one of the most successful business women in America. This selection was based on women who had demonstrated outstanding achievements in their own fields of endeavor, and had contributed significantly to the betterment of a contemporary society.

• *New York Times*– Featured many times in articles regarding my inspiring sales achievements in the textile industry.

• *Daily News-Record* – Featured many times in the Menswear trade publication, which focused on clothing and breaking news in the men's and women's fashion industries.

• *Women's Wear Daily* – Womenswear trade publication that is sometimes known as the "Bible of Women Fashions." I was featured in many articles for my creative and innovative fashion concepts.

Received many awards and trophies for outstanding entrepreneur sales achievements.While working at Burlington Industries, I made sure that I attended every training seminar that the company offered on selling skills and techniques. I completed a two-year program in advertising and marketing at FIT (Fashion Institute of Technology) which is an internationally recognized College of Fashion, Communication, Business, Advertising and Marketing that is located in New York City. I took advantage of learning everything I could about the business world because my long-term goal was to own my own business. Every year, I would travel to three or four of the "HBCU" Historical Black Colleges and Universities to interview and hire three students for the Summer Internship Program that I set up at Burlington Industries. This was a paid, ten-week program designed to expose, engage and educate the students by giving them tangible and real-world experience... It was exciting and rewarding to be able to help Black students jump-start their careers in the field of sales and marketing in the textile industries.

The years at Burlington Industries were very challenging. However, I managed to overcome most of the obstacles and roadblocks, and had a very successful and rewarding career where I was able to break down the barriers of a woman selling in an all-man's world and was able to open doors for other women to enter the textile industry at the sale executive level. I had a chance to prove that women can sell textile fabrics, or any product, if they are committed, dedicated, and willing to work hard to reach their ultimate goal. One of my greatest accomplishments was being able to open up the Designer Menswear market, which added millions of dollars to Burlington Industries' bottom line. People often ask me if I had to deal with sexual harassment? The answer is "Yes," but during that period of time it was not something that you would generally report to the Human Resource Department. Simply because it was a man's world, and the world that I wanted to be part of. I knew upfront that I would have to take on this challenge. Therefore, I learned how to handle it myself.

When I was first hired by Burlington Industries in the early 1970s there were no women in sales at most of your Fortune 500 companies. Years later, most companies were seeking to hire women, especially those who had been trailblazers with other companies. When you had reached the stage of development that I had, the field was wide open. Not a week went past that I didn't receive a job offer from another company. I quickly told them that I was not interested in making a career change. I thought that I had carved out a career for myself at Burlington, and expected a promotion to a corporate executive level, and a longtime career. One day, I got a call from the executive vice president of Avon Products wanting to know if I would be interested in making a career change into the cosmetic industry. I told him "No." He called again a few days later, and I said "No." However, on the third call, he said they were very impressed with the career successes that I had in my current position, and would like to meet with me. After giving it some consideration, I agreed to meet with him to learn more about the company. I didn't know much about Avon Products, Inc. Therefore, I needed to do some market research quickly to learn more about Avon's past and future. After some extensive research, to my surprise, I learned that Avon Products was a direct sales company in beauty, household, and personal care products. They were the largest cosmetic company globally, larger than Revlon, and all the other cosmetic companies. They had over $3 billion in sales and more than 1.4 million sales representatives in over thirty countries. They were the second-largest direct-selling enterprise globally (after Amway), and the company's headquarters was located in New York City. They had just purchased Tiffany & Company and had plans to make it the flagship of its specialty retail division.

Chapter Nine
Business Strategies for Success

After doing my market research, I found all the data about Avon Products to be positive. I was interested in learning more about the company and why they were so interested in talking to me. I called and scheduled an appointment to meet with the Vice President, not realizing that I would be meeting with six of the corporate executives, including the President of the company.

During my meeting, I learned that the 1970s had brought some of the most challenging times in Avon's history. Sales growth had stalled. They had been hit hard by the recession, with over 25,000 sales representatives quitting. They had recently brought in a new CEO/President to revive and rejuvenate the company earnings. Avon's earnings had been suffering from the slow growth in cosmetics and door-to-door sales marketing maturing. The new CEO/President immediately wanted to restructure and revamp the company making it a leaner, more efficient, more results and profit-oriented company while retaining the emphasis on caring, which had been the company's trademark since 1886. The President's goal was to reverse a decade of declining sales and change the way women thought of Avon and its products. His commitment was to bring in a top executive sales manager from outside the company with new innovative sales ideas, concepts, and marketing techniques that would motivate the sales field. He wanted to hire someone who had a proven track record, and had the necessary skills needed to get the job done. Which was to reverse the slumping sales, and to change the way women thought of Avon and its products. Avon traditionally was a company that had promoted from within, which is good but sometimes not good.

The day of interviewing was very stressful. I met with six corporate executives and the CEO/President, and had an opportunity to learn more about Avon's past, present and goals for future growth. I didn't have to share much about myself; they had done their homework, and were up to date about my sales career successes. They were very impressed with my background, and the impact that I had on creating and opening up the designer menswear market, and the overall sales results it produced for Burlington Industries.

After the initial meeting, they said they would get back to me in a couple of days. Three days later, I received a call from the Vice President. They offered me a newly created position as the National Field Sales Manager of a new department, called Motivation/Recognition, and I would be working out of the New York headquarters. The salary they offered was almost double the salary that I was making, and I was already making an excellent salary. This new position had been approved by senior management and the board of directors. I would be the first person hired at this level from outside the company. Traditionally, Avon promoted from within, but now they wanted to bring in someone with new innovated ideas and concepts to help motivate the sales team and rejuvenate the company's sales. I thanked them for the job offer and told them that I would like to take a few days to think about it before making a decision.

I realized that I needed to understand more about their marketing and sales operation before I would be able to put together a program that would motivate a sales team of 100 Division Sales Managers, 2,100 District Sales Managers, who are employees of the company, and over 500,000 Sales Representatives in the United States. I needed to know more about the sales field operation from the ground floor up to the corporate level, and have a clearer understanding of what the job involved, who I would report to, and where I would fall on the corporate ladder. I learned that the Division and District Sales Managers are salaried employees, and that the Sales Representatives are Independent Contractors that reported to the District Sales Managers, who report to the Division Sales Managers, who report to the Regional Sales Managers, who report to the National Sales Managers, who reported to the Vice President of Sales. I wanted to make sure that they knew that I was looking for a long-term career with upward mobility, and not be stuck in a dead-end position. I wanted to know how profitable the company was and what were their future plans for expansion over the next five years. After obtaining this information, I began plotting my plan to maximize my potential, making them even more anxious to hire me, while giving myself time to weigh my decision objectively, and by playing a little hard to get, which would make me even more valuable.

I loved the concept that over 100 years ago, Avon was the first company to give women a chance to earn money in sales even before they could vote. Being an Avon Sales Representative is about freedom and owning your own business. Avon's history was built on caring, and everybody had heard of "Avon Calling." Their products were rated as outstanding, and I was happy to know that the new executive management team wanted to reinvent the company's image without eliminating their caring heritage.

A week later, I set up an appointment to meet with Avon's management team to go over my plans. I shared with them that the only way I could successfully put together a plan and a program to help them to turn the sales around would be to have a clearer understanding of why sales were decreasing and not growing as projected. I would need to spend time working in the sales field with the Division Sales Managers, District Sales Managers, and the Sales Representatives to learn more about what had caused the decrease in sales. I would need to know more about their products, and sales operation from the ground floor up to the corporate level. I felt that finding a solution to what was causing this tremendous decrease in sales would require hands-on management at the sales field level. Sales are the core of Avon's business, and they got the vast majority of their 650 products to the consumers through its familiar "Avon Calling!" Using Sales Representatives through a systemized sales network, second to no other direct sales company in the world. I laid out my complete plan: Which was to relocate to the Cincinnati Regional Branch Headquarters for two years as a Division Sales Manager to learn more about the inner workings of the sales field operations, and to focus on what had caused a decrease in sales, and how to fix it. I would need to have a guaranteed contract stating that at the end of two years, I would be relocated back to the Home Office in New York City, and promoted to Executive National Field Sales Manager of Motivation and Recognition, which would be a new department responsible for all incentives and recognition programs for the entire United States sales team. My next step was to negotiate my salary, and other fringe benefits for an executive, i.e., relocation package, expense account, stock option, health insurance, and vacation.

After all the details were worked out, I accepted the position of Division Sales Manager and was the first Black woman hired at that level. My next step was to fly out to Cincinnati for a few days to find an apartment. I would need to find one that was near the airport because I would be traveling a lot. After looking at a lot of apartments, I finally found a townhouse with three bedrooms in Hyde Park called Regency Square that would be great for myself, my daughter in college, and my son at a private boarding school back east. It was perfect. It reminded me of the high-rise condominium where I had lived on East 72nd Street in

New York City, it had a doorman and twenty-four-hour security. Because I traveled so much, I thought I would feel comfortable and protected there. I immediately leased the townhouse and packed up and relocated to Hyde Park where I would be working out of the Cincinnati, Ohio Regional office for the next two years. My division would cover part of the state of Michigan, and accounted for over $11.5 million in annual sales for the company

The division was composed of 21 District Sales Managers, and over 4,000 Sales Representatives. Each District Sales Manager directed a sales force of about 200-250 representatives generating revenue of about $1 million. Their responsibilities included prospecting, appointing, training and development of new representatives, my primary responsibility was to hire and train the District Sales Managers, which would involve many training meetings, and working with each manager in their market to observe their daily activities in order to give them constructive feedback to help them grow and develop their management, recruiting and selling skills. In order to accomplish this goal, I would need to spend about 70 percent of my time traveling and working with each manager doing training seminars and monthly staff meetings. This would allow me to learn more about Avon's business, what was causing the decline in sales, and what needed to be done to motivate the sales team, and put the company back on track showing sales increases.

My goal over the next two years was to increase sales in the Division from $11.5 million to $21.5 million by focusing on training, motivating and recognizing the District Sales Managers, and Sales Representatives for their sales performance. This would be accomplished by setting small attainable weekly, monthly and quarterly goals, where each District Sales Manager, and Sales Representative would be able to stretch a little, but not having a goal that seemed totally unreachable. I wanted to make sure that I kept in mind the old saying, "How do you eat an elephant? One bite at a time!" The goals that I needed to set for the Division, District Sales Managers and Sales Representatives would be an aggressive sales increase. To achieve this sales goal, I would need to know exactly where I wanted to take the sales team step by step. It would mean being creative, and taking a thorough look at the existing sales practices, then translating them into my own course of action, which would mean not doing things the way they had always been done. It was important that I worked directly with the managers and representatives to learn from the bottom up about the Field Sales Operations of Avon Products. I would need to find out what was causing the continuous decline in sales, and what had to be done to turn sales around, and put the company back on track showing a sales increase.

Avon's greatest strength was its people, because not only were they in the cosmetic business, they were also in the people business. Therefore, as a people-oriented company, their job was to offer women an opportunity to enrich their lives by following the principles of Avon which was to encourage everyone to grow and reach their full potential. Because without the Sales Representatives, there would be no Avon Products. Over time the company, people, and the products may change, but what's important is that the company's philosophy remains intact. It's that quality that determines the greatness of an organization. In any company, it is the sales team that takes precedence over all other divisions of the company, because the dollar intake from the sales is the life-blood of all the different departments/divisions of the company. The more productive the salespeople are, the more profitable and powerful the company becomes. Sales was the core of Avon, because the company got its vast array of products (more than 650 marketed domestically) to the consumers through its familiar "Avon Calling!" Avon had been in direct selling since 1886, and had developed a systemized sales network second to no other direct sellers in the world.

After working a short period of time with the Sales Representatives, I quickly learned that one of the main things that the company had been built on was placing emphasis on "Caring" which had been Avon's trademark since 1886. But over the years, with the expansion and growth of the company, the District Sale Manager and Sales Representatives felt the company had lost "Caring" about them. They thought that the harder they worked, the less recognition they received.

Avon's Sales Representatives team was made up of about 95 percent independent businesswomen who enjoyed interaction with other people to help supplement their family income, be their own boss, and work from home. Many women felt that "Oh, I could never sell," what they were really saying is, "I don't have enough self-confidence." Typically, women crave praise and need it for self-confidence. Women want to be recognized for their achievements, and it is recognition that gives them self-confidence; therefore, they will work for an award because everyone loves to be admired and recognized. Most women that choose a career in sales find the rewards are well worth the efforts.

I learned that women love to compete for recognition, especially when competing with themselves, and where everyone has an opportunity to be recognized. In putting together incentive programs to motivate the sales team, I would need to avoid designing programs where each person has to compete with everyone else, and there is only one winner. I believed that any competition is more productive when you are competing with yourself. Making the desire for recognition a powerful motivator; therefore, it was crucial that I created the right incentive programs, and chose suitable prizes that women would love to have, i.e.; (trips, rubies, pearls and diamonds) which would be a great form of recognition to help build self-esteem and show that "caring spirit."

Chapter Ten
Setting Goals

As a Division Sales Manager, my responsibility was to train, develop and motivate twenty-one District Sales Managers, and 4,000 Sales Representatives focusing primarily on what was causing the slump in corporate sales. The first thing that I needed to focus on was training, which would be done at monthly training seminars, staff meetings, and working with each manager in their markets to observe their daily activities and give them constructive feedback to help them grow and develop. The training would consist of developing a strategic plan, focusing on marketing and motivational techniques. The focus of the training would be on the four critical selling skills: Time Management, Setting Goals, Recruiting and Motivation/Recognition:

Time Management – Which is a skill that is necessary for success in sales. Knowing how to manage your time can make or break you because time is too precious to be wasted. I've always been time-conscious. Knowing that there are only twenty-four hours in a day, I've tried to get the most mileage out of those hours. Statistic shows that people with good time management skills usually get great sales results. Having good time management skills can help you plan and exercise control of the time you spend on specific activities. Especially in helping you to know how to increase effectiveness, efficiency, and productivity.

Setting Goals – Without goals, you can waste your life with nothing to show for it but a feeling of frustration and dissatisfaction. To accomplish anything, you must sit down and decide what you want from life. Knowing what your short and long-term goals are because without a plan and a road map, you will never get to where you want to go. It helps to visualize your goals by writing them down. It is vital that you set realistic short-term goals that you can actually attain and then go on to long-term goals. Your goals should always be broken into small segments: daily, weekly, monthly, quarterly, and annually. I taught each of them how to use the "SMART GOAL" concept to set goals for their districts, which would help them get great sales results: (S) SPECIFIC - be clear and concise. (M) MEASURABLE - make sure your goals are measurable. (A) ATTAINABLE - make sure your goals are achievable. (R) RELEVANT - Make sure they are realistic. (T) TIME-BOUND - make sure there is a set deadline to reach each goal. Learn how to master these goal-setting skills will set each of them up for success and give them a clear goal to work towards.

Recruiting – Is the process of attracting, interviewing, selecting and bringing in new Sales Representatives, which is the first step needed to create a robust resource sales base, which is the heart of the company, "Its people." The training should focus on the following areas: attention to details, advertising, referrals, marketing, relationship building, and listening skills, and all District Sales Managers should have good communication skills, because they are the critical link between the Sales Representatives and the company.

Motivation Recognition – For me to improve the division's success, it would mean making motivation/recognition a priority because a motivated sales team is critical to the overall success of the division and the company. The relationship that is built with the sales team creates the company's foundation – not just in individual sales, but in overall reputation and growth, which will affect productivity, culture, and the bottom line.

It was my responsibility to keep the sales managers engaged and be fully supportive of their districts' mission. I started by working with each of them to find out what would work best for their district. I explained what the division goals would mean to their districts, and how they each played a part. I decided to start by giving each of them a short-term goal, so they would not be overwhelmed by a long-term goal. As the saying goes, "How do you eat an elephant, One bite at a time."

My next goal was to work on building trust because it is the foundation of motivation. If the sales team doesn't trust you and believe you have their best interests at heart, it'll be difficult for them to feel inspired and driven by their work. I focused on having a helping mindset in order to help them solve problems and support the sales team growth. My goal was to create a comfortable environment where each of them would feel appreciated and engaged.

The main difference between good companies and great companies is their recognition programs. Most sales companies have some type of recognition program. They're usually branded with elite names like "President Club," or "Peak Performers." These recognition programs are typically designed for the top performers. When I think of recognition programs, I believe that, "Good companies recognize top performers' accomplishments, and great companies tell the stories of top performers." Therefore, a meaningful and robust recognition program will show the sales team how important they are to the organization. Great recognition programs can play an even more critical function for the entire sales team by communicating your corporate culture, valves, and the importance that the company places on its people. Recognition programs should be designed to award the sales team for performance across multiple areas.

To ignore the performance of sales people, is almost as bad as shredding their sales efforts in front of their face.

Everyone wants to be recognized for doing a great job. The best way to recognize inspiring participants' loyalty can be accomplished through tangible awards keeping in mind that not all sales people are motivated by the same thing. My goal was to develop top sales performers by combining different recognition programs to keep all of the sales team motivated. There are many various recognition programs, I decided to use the "Fun" award route with sales contests, i.e., weekend trips for two, dinner for two, cold cash and other innovative rewards. I put together a Group Sales Team competition that was very successful because the sales managers were not competing as individuals, but as a team. For a team to win the battle, they would have to rely on and push each other to perform. What was even more exciting was how many of the Sales Representatives wanted to help their managers win. The winning team and other top performers were recognized at the monthly staff meetings in front of their peers. This team competition helped to build camaraderie, and lend itself to helping with kindness and fairness, and just by saying these words every day, which everyone loves to hear, "Thank you," for your hard work and a job well done. Verbal recognition is clearly the most effective way to recognize a person, but the best way is at a sales meeting in front of their peers. I would often surprise the sales team and take them out for an unscheduled lunch at a five-star restaurant to celebrate a job well done. By offering a variety of rewards, I stood a greater chance of having a motivator for every sales member and developing all the sales managers into top sales performers. This can happen when your "goals and your sales team goals align," because "motivation through recognition can and does work."

Long-term goals can sometimes seem overwhelming, but as the old Chinese proverb goes, "The longest journey begins with a single step." In other words, to accomplish great things, you must achieve one small goal at a time. It was important that I set realistic short-term goals that they could actually reach, then go on to bigger goals as they gained confidence in their ability. I believed that "goals should scare you a little, and excite you a lot." The key to success is to learn to "Think Big, and then think bigger than that." I knew that once they had achieved their goal, they would get a sense of purpose that would inspire them to work harder, and inspire their loyalty. Statistics show that people who love their job usually tend to do better. I continuously emphasize – what they get by reaching their goals is not nearly as important as what they become.

Each manager's goal was to do the best they could each day, while preparing for a better tomorrow, knowing that the future is the place where they would spend the rest of their life. Their daily accomplishments should be like steps with bricks that lead to their long-term goal, and if they regularly and firmly put the bricks into place each day, they would eventually build their stairway to the top. In order for each of them to reach their long-term goal, they would need to clearly understand that the elevator to the top was, "Out of Order." Therefore, they would need to take the stairs – one step at a time in order to achieve their long-term goals.

Most people don't realize that the real opportunity for success lies within the person and not in the job. They don't realize that success and happiness are not matters of choice, but you choose what you want in life. My responsibility as Division Sales Manager was to work with each of the Sales Managers to help them set meaningful, reachable goals, and to help remove the obstacles that kept them from performing their job. I saw my role as being there to train, support, and do whatever was necessary to help them develop and grow. Each Sales Manager's needs were different, so management became a highly personalized endeavor where some days I felt like a psychologist, trying to read each manager's individual needs, and how to respond to them. My goal was to try to make work fun, and to personally recognize each of them for a job well done.

I had learned the importance of being a good listener as a young girl from my grandmother who would never repeat anything twice. Therefore, I learned early in life to be a good listener, and I believe that having good listening skills is one of the most important selling skills that a sales person can have. Learning to be a good listener is critical, and I stressed it often to the Sales Managers. As a wise man once said, "Talking is sharing but listening is caring," and Avon places its emphasis on "caring" which has been their trademark.

I taught each of the managers the importance of having good eye contact when having a conversation, by looking their peers and associates in the eye at every opportunity. This procedure would help them to build their self-image because the way they see themselves will determine who they are. They should start by asking themselves, is self-image important? The answer is yes, because you cannot consistently perform in a manner that is inconsistent with the way you see yourself. It is your self-image that will lead you to the top of the stairs, by learning to see yourself as a deserving person, and then you can be successful. The starting point for success and happiness starts with a positive self-image. Having a strong positive self-image is the best possible preparation for success in life. "You must feel that you deserve success, and happiness, before it will happen."

I continually stressed and reminded them, that "Success is easy – once you believe," and that they could have everything they wanted, if they helped enough people get what they wanted, and by helping each other they help themselves, because the way we see situations and people is extremely important, and it helps to avoid treating people and situations as we see them.

Setting sales goals gave the sales team a clear road map of what they needed to do to help their district, division, and the company. Goals are usually long-term goals, made up of short-term goals. Remember there's a difference between setting sales objectives, and setting sales objectives that work. Just because you plan something doesn't mean it will work. That is why sales objectives that have a chance of succeeding need to be done in steps, and that is why I worked with each manager to help them break down their annual sales goals into quarterly, monthly, weekly, and daily.

I challenged myself, and the sales team to meet their weekly goals by posting their progress, and rewarding top performers with small weekly prizes such as a gift certificate to a nice restaurant to share dinner with a loved one. Each week, I would review the districts and the division goals, and evaluate what was working to increase sales, and what wasn't. Having sales goals help to ensure that the sales team is driven, on-task, and producing sales that will impact the bottom line. It ensures that sales are constantly improving and growing, and, most importantly showing a sales boost in revenue. Having sales goals was critical to the overall success of the districts, division and the company. These sales goals helped to ensure that each manager was motivated and focused on hitting their goals, which allowed me to evaluate the success of the sales team as a whole, and the individual sales managers who made up the team. Ultimately, it's all about sales growth, and in order to drive sales growth, sales goals need to be challenging and realistic – lofty but attainable. Achieving a goal isn't a slam dunk. Ask yourself can you do what it takes to make your goals? Making sure that your goals are clear because "without clear goals, you will not be able to see your progress, you will lose your momentum, and you won't be able to see if the training is paying off."

In my experience, only two things set apart those who live by goals and those who don't. Sales people who live by goals (1.) Know where they are going and (2.) are committed to achieving their goals. Reaching your goals is only the beginning, and must always remain the beginning, because success and happiness are not destinations, they're exciting, never-ending journeys. Your beginning puts you in a position of being both a "go-getter," which you are, and a "go-giver," which you're beginning to become. The key for me was to be hands-on while giving each of them the room they needed to succeed on their own. In order for me to motivate the sales team, their goals needed to be meaningful and effective, and they needed to understand the role they played in the overall success of the division and the company, so they would not become disengaged.

It's common knowledge that helping the sales team set and reach goals was a critical part of my job. The sales team wanted to know how their districts contributed to the company's objectives, and setting the right targets made this connection clear for them, and for myself. Goal-setting is particularly important and is a way for providing ongoing and year-end feedback. By establishing and monitoring targets, I was able to give the sales team real-time input on their performance, while motivating them to achieve their goal. The main two things that I focused on were how to increase motivation for each manager (inspiring them to work harder through setting goals, and creating incentives), and increasing the efficacy of their efforts through training and skill development, while setting the stage for organizational and operational success, and creating an environment for myself and the sales team to do our best work.

As each District Sales Manager reached their weekly, monthly, or quarterly goals, I would share these updates with them so they could see progress, and would recognize their success at an upcoming staff meeting in front of their peers. This was a great way to boost morale and keep them engaged. Celebrating their success encouraged a culture of camaraderie, and when the division reached its goals, everyone had a chance to celebrate making them feel like they were part of the success. This created an environment that was positive, and promoted applauding each other which helped to bring the sales team closer towards reaching their goal. Everyone likes to be recognized for their efforts, and feel appreciated and rewarded for their hard work. That's why it was important that I had a sales contest that was done right, so it would inspire the sales team to tackle their goals head-on. I learned that just a sincere compliment was one of the most effective teaching and motivational methods in existence, and I used it often.

It was my responsibility to set the stage for organizational and operational success. By recognizing the value of communication, coaching, training and development which helped to define what success looks like. Defining success is a key responsibility for effective managers, and when you can't or won't define it, you can bet your bottom dollars they aren't going to work to help achieve the goal. The District Sales Managers are the difference between success and failure, between high and low morale, and between a thriving sales environment and a toxic one. My objective was to be hands-on, while giving them the room they needed to succeed on their own, by making sure they each had a clear understanding of the bigger picture, and the role that their district played in the company's overall success.

I spent the next twelve months training and motivating the District Sales Managers who were responsible for recruiting, training, and motivating the Sales Representatives in their district. Once a month, I would hold a large division sales meeting for all the District Sales Managers and Sales Representatives to introduce new products and recognize top sales performers for each district. These meetings gave me an opportunity to get to know who the top sales performers were in the division and be able to personally recognize them for their outstanding sales performance. The Sales Representatives are bombarded by outside factors every day, that was affecting their motivation. Their customers might be telling them, "No," over and over again, or there may be some other disaster going on that is affecting their ability to sell. In order for them to be successful they needed to be hyped up and ready to go at all times, because a lack of motivation from the Sales Representatives affects productivity and the bottom line. Therefore, if I was going to improve the sales success of the division, I would need to focus on training and motivation as a top priority.

Traveling 70 percent of the time, staying at hotels during a time when traveling was still a new thing for executive business women, was challenging. My secretary would always try to book me at the same hotel usually getting the same room on a high floor which made me feel more at home. She would book large conference rooms for staff meetings and other business activities. This gave me an opportunity to get to know the hotel sales staff and get special VIP treatment. In order to be ready to take off at a moment's notice, I always kept one bag perpetually packed, and in it was an extra set of cosmetics, hairdryer, pantyhose and lingerie. All I needed to do each week was to grab a couple of pantsuits, silk blouses, and put them in my hanging bag, and I was off for the airport. I settled for using pantsuits as my all-occasion "uniform." Pantsuits were the answer because there were not a lot of women traveling, and they gave me a professional business look and the more professional I appeared, the more I was accepted.

After six months of training and hard work, the division was beginning to show a sales increase. To make sure we stayed on track of achieving our goals, it was essential to constantly monitor the progress of the districts and division, which gave me an overview of how much was done and how much more was left to do. Achieving individual district goals is what would determine the overall success of how committed each District Sales Manager was to reaching their individual goals, and what they were willing to sacrifice in order to achieve their goals. I knew that if they kept their focus on the excitement of learning, improving and exploring, they would find themselves fully committed and motivation would follow. The key to their overall success was for them to focus on the journey, not the destination.

Everyone's daily goal was to do the best they could while preparing for a better tomorrow, and as they set their goals their first step was to develop a positive self-image. The second step was to recognize the worth and ability of other people. The third step was to have a strong goal orientation, and they must have a lot of "want to." I would emphasize that what they get by reaching their goals was not nearly as important as what they become, and that they should always follow their dreams and ambitions. Don't let their friends and associates make negative comments about their dreams and goals, making them become a SNIOP, which mean a person who is Susceptible to the Negative Influence of Other People.

As the sales team completed projects and hit sales milestones, I shared with them updates showing where they were tracking toward reaching their individual or district goals. Everyone could see progress, and we celebrated their hard work and success by recognizing their achievements at sales meetings or at a special celebration. By recognizing the entire sales team for its contributions toward achieving their district's goals helped to motivate each individual to continue to excel in their sales role. This was a great way for boosting morale and keeping everyone engaged. I truly believe that life is too short not to have fun. The more fun you are having, the more you will want to work toward achieving your goals.

At the end of the first year, the division had a 40 percent sales increase which was right on target for the first year's sales projection. All the training, motivating and overall hard work was beginning to pay off and most of the twenty-one districts were showing a sales increase. The morale among the District Sale Managers and Sales Representatives was high. They were excited and motivated which inspired them to work harder toward achieving their goals. They liked being recognized for their sales achievements, and were able to see the impact of their hard work and how it contributed to their district, division and the company's overall sales objectives.

In my second year, I began cutting my traveling time down to about 60 percent on the road and 40 percent in the office, in order to have more time to begin working on putting together a Motivation Recognition program for the entire Avon Corporate sales team which was composed of 2100 District Sales Managers, and over 400,000 Avon Sales Representatives in the United States. I had learned a lot the first year working in the field, hands-on with the managers and representatives. I learned why Avon's sales were decreasing, and had a clearer understanding of what needed to be done in order to help fix the current morale problems and boost the company's sales. As a Division Sales Manager, part of my responsibility was to manage other people, which can be a difficult task because you have your own emotions to content, and the emotions of your sales team. At this point management is a highly personalized endeavor where you must be a psychologist knowing how to read each person's needs, and how to respond to them. My goal was to help them to continue to set meaningful reachable goals, and be able to help them remove any obstacles that would keep them from achieving their goals. I wanted to be supportive and to do whatever was necessary to help them grow, develop, and to make work fun by personally rewarding, recognizing and praising them for their sales efforts.

I continued with the extensive training seminars, motivation, and recognition programs, teaching the managers how to develop a strong belief in themselves and their products through enhancing, reinforcing, and practicing the following:Don't wish for less problems; wish for more results.Don't wish for less challenges, wish for more wisdom.Don't wish it was easier; wish you were better.

I reminded them that what they are thinking today will determine what and where they will be tomorrow. If they replaced negative thoughts with positive thoughts, they will feel better, and have more confidence, by becoming a self-motivated person that is self-driven, and constantly competing with his or herself, and always striving to be the best. We set goals to give our lives focus and to move in the direction we want to go. If you don't know what you want or where you are going, you will end up nowhere because "If you fail to plan – you plan to fail." (Walt Disney). This quote is about dreaming great and beautiful things, and making them so powerful in your head that you simply can make them come to life, if you have the courage to pursue them. In order for me to continue to help the sales team grow and succeed, I listened to their feedback so I would be able to provide invaluable insight. I would often remind them that it's not the occupation or profession that makes you succeed or fail, it's how you see yourself that will allow you to continue to grow, mature and excel. That they should avoid being like people who are always looking for the magic, but fail to realize that the magic is within themselves.

Since I was traveling less, I began to do more networking and socializing in the beautiful city of Cincinnati, which was a very vibrant community with plenty of things to do and places to go. It was a food lover's paradise, and home to nine companies that are on the Fortune 500 list, i.e., Proctor Gamble, Federal Stores and Kroger Corporation, and there were companies like IBM, Xerox, and General Motors that had major offices located here. Most of the people that I met and socialized with were relocated from other cities and states. There were a lot of IBM employees, and we formed a little group and called ourselves the "I Been Moved," because IBM was known to relocate their employees. We had great times together and became very good friends. This is where I met my future husband, he was from a small town in Louisiana, and had graduated from Southern University with a degree in Electrical Engineering. He was an Assistant Zone Sales Manager with General Motors. At that time, I was not interested in dating someone in Cincinnati, and I was not looking for a husband, my goal was to spend two years in Cincinnati, be promoted to the next executive sales level and relocated back to New York City where I loved living and working, and this is where my friends lived.

At the end of two years my mission as a Division Sales Manager had been accomplished. I had achieved my ultimate sales goal for the division, which was to increase sales from $11.5 million to $21.5 million. We did it. All twenty-one District Sales Managers had achieved their sales goals, and all of the Sales Representatives were excited about their personal sales growth and achievements. They felt like their sales achievements had made them an important part of the Avon organization.

◇

Chapter Eleven
Succeeding in Sales

I was promoted to Field Sales Manager of Motivation/Recognition which was a new department where I would be responsible for creating and designing new programs to motivate and recognize the entire United States sales team. I would be relocating back to New York City to work out of the Avon Corporate headquarters located on 57th Avenue. The promotion came with a big increase in salary, a lot of extra fringe benefits, and a great relocation package. All of the division sales team was excited and elated for me. They felt like they had played an important role in my success and promotion. At the last sales staff meeting that I conducted for the sales team, I shared these remarks. I reminded them that having a career in sales can be tough. Why? Because you are always working with objectives and goals, and no matter how good you were last month or last year you are expected to be better this year. Therefore, you are constantly striving to beat "your best," and that is why having good sales skills is critical. I told them that I hoped that the time we had spent together during the past two years had helped them to grow, develop and excel.

I reminded them that winning starts with beginning. Because success is the result of good judgement, good judgement is the result of experience, and experience is often the result of bad judgement. I asked each of them to continue to look in the mirror, and ask themselves if they are the person that they want to be? And to always remember that all things are possible if they just believe in themselves, and no matter how much they have achieved to keep looking for more, and always believe that tomorrow will be better, even though today has been great. I thanked the entire sales team that had worked so hard to get to this day. I shared with them that all the new incentive/recognition programs that I create and design would be with them in mind, because they had played an important role in the development of these new incentive programs. I assured them that they could feel free to call me anytime, and I gave them my new phone number.

I closed my last staff meeting with two of my favorite quotes from Maya Angelou and Ralph Waldo Emerson respectively. "You may encounter many defeats, but you must not be defeated." In fact, it may be necessary to encounter the defeats, so you can know who you are, what you can rise from, and how you can still come out of it, because, "You cannot do a kindness too soon, for you will never know how soon it will be too late."

On the road again. After being promoted it was now time to pack up and relocate back to New York City. Destination – Avon Corporate Headquarters. I had a lot to do, I needed to sell the townhouse that I had purchased in Cincinnati, and find a place to live in New York City. My relocation package gave me two weeks off to accomplish some of the things I needed to do prior to relocating and starting a new position and department. I was so excited, and at the same time overwhelmed with the idea of facing new challenges which I knew I could handle, since I believed in myself, and had lived and worked in New York City at Burlington Industries Corporate Headquarters which was only a few blocks from Avon's Corporate Headquarters.

Once back in New York my first objective was to find a place to live. I started my search immediately because living in a hotel was no fun. It was a real challenge finding a place because I was looking for a new luxury high rise condominium with a view. After weeks of looking, I did find the perfect place. It was called Harmon Cove Towers, which had a large balcony that overlooked the Hudson River. The condominium that I purchased was on a high floor with a large balcony that had a fantastic view of the New York City skyline, and the Hudson River. It had twenty-four-hour doorman service and underground parking. Thankfully, the townhouse that I owned in Cincinnati sold quickly, and I was able to purchase the new condominium. I made immediate plans with the moving company to relocate my household items, and I moved into my new place. I loved the new condominium that was very accessible to work and play.

After getting settled into my new place, it was now time to really focus on my new position. The first thing I needed to do was to get my new office set up and hire six people. The first person I hired was my former secretary from Burlington Industries who had outstanding administration skills. I offered her a new career opportunity as an Administrative Assistant with an increase in salary. She accepted the position, and I was very pleased because she understood my work ethics, and my personality. She was an outstanding person and we worked well together. I hired five other people to make up my new department team of seven, which I called the "Lucky Seven." My goal was to create a workplace committed to encouraging happiness, productivity, and a dynamic culture, where each could look forward to being part of an outstanding team.

I began to work on putting together a new innovated recognition program that would change the course and direction of Avon, and help put them back on track for reaching their projected sales goals. The first thing that I wanted to focus on was what I called "people power," because the direct selling business is resoundingly unscientific, primarily because the buying and selling decisions are dependent on the unpredictable behavior of people. All goals and objectives that are established must be accomplished through the efforts of the sales field team who has a direct or indirect impact on sales. In order to accomplish this goal, I realized that I would need to create and design a planned motivational program that would offer both long and short-term incentive programs to effectively influence, motivate and recognize top sales performers. This new recognition program would be done through creating and entering into a "Nu-Era of Achievement," designed to motivate and recognize sales performers.

My primary objective was to create and sustain a "Go for it attitude" that would be single focused and sensational in its rewards. It would uplift the sales team to new heights of effort and self-esteem, and reward those that can perform and change sluggishness into enthusiasm and excitement in order to generate higher sales. To achieve this goal, I designed a new motivational program that would focus on their individual basic motives, personal gain, desire for recognition, avoidance of boredom, pride and family involvement. These five basic motives would provide the keys to opening the doors to unlimited sales potential. Instead of a yearly motivational program, I chose to go with quarterly recognition programs to ensure high enthusiasm throughout the year, and provide a second opportunity for those who missed one or two quarterly sales objectives. This new motivational program would have continuity and recognized the top and above average sales achievers by allowing them an opportunity to select the prize of their choice from the new "Avon Quest for Excellence" award book, and they would receive a special signed congratulatory letter from the president of the company. My goal was to increase the District Sales Managers recognition program, from recognizing the top 10 percent to the top 20 percent by creating a new "Circle of Achievement" program, and enhancing the "Circle of Excellence" travel award program with exclusive recognition jewelry that I designed and had custom made by Tiffany's. At that time, Avon owned Tiffany's. These two programs would offer increased recognition, which would help to expand the company's motivational impact and sales. I would introduce two new programs, "President's Club" and "The New Spirit of Avon." These programs would recognize and reward the achievements of outstanding Sales Representatives, and both programs would have a new look – and a new format. Representatives that reached these sales levels would join a prestigious group, and these new enhanced programs would be one of the most challenging, comprehensive and exciting incentive programs ever offered for Sales Representatives, where they would want to let the "New Spirit of Avon" take them higher than ever before. Once they became a member of "The President's Club" they would receive the Mrs. Albee Award at the Annual Awards Celebration to mark their outstanding sales achievements. I designed a beautiful new fine porcelain statuette that would depict Mrs. P.F.E. Albee, who was Avon's first woman Sales Representative in the early 1800s. The Mrs. Albee award was a highly collectible series, and a different one was awarded exclusively to President's Club members each year.

The "New Spirit of Avon" offered some exciting new recognition programs, i.e., Award Gift Catalog, U.S. Saving Bonds, and the annual President's Club recognition pin that I worked with Tiffany's to design. In order to beautifully interpret the feeling of reaching new heights, the joy of achievements, and that special feeling of going as far as you want to go. There were four different variations of the beautiful 14K gold pin, each corresponding to a different sales level. Each pin ranged from one beautiful ruby stone to four which was determined by your sales. The higher the sales, the more precious ruby stones your 14K gold pin had.

My next step was to create a new "Anniversary Awards Program" that would recognize the Sales Representatives with thirty to fifty years of service, and remind them of how very special they are to the company. It didn't take long to know that women love diamonds and pearls. So once again, I worked with Tiffany's to design a beautiful collection of jewelry, with shimmering pearls, sparkling diamonds, and glowing 14K gold that would be a true tribute to those whose association was highly valued and treasured by Avon.

• 30 Years – An elegant 14K Gold Rose Bud Pin with a diamond.
• 35 Years – 14K Gold Rose Bud Earrings with a diamond.
• 40 Years – A double strand Tiffany Pearl Bracelet with a 14K Gold Rose Bud Clasp with a diamond.
• 45 Years – 20" Strand of Tiffany Pearls, with a 14K Gold Rose Bud with a diamond
• 50 Years – 14K Gold Tiffany watch with diamonds.

Avon had always placed great value on Sales Representatives who had been associated with the company for many years, and they hoped that these special awards would be a reminder as to how special they are., The Sales Representatives were very excited, and the new Anniversary Awards Program was overwhelmingly successful.

After spending two years in Cincinnati analyzing the sales team and sales results. I had learned that sales at Avon were decreasing across the United States because the Representatives and Managers felt that Avon had lost that "caring" feeling, and that they were not being recognized for their sales efforts. I knew that the first thing I needed to do was to find a way to change that misconception, and assure them that the company did care. After giving it a lot of thought, I came up with a great idea that would get their attention, and would represent caring and growing. After extensive research, I found a nursery in Florida that would ship a small live "Palm Tree" to over 400,000 Sales Representatives from the President of Avon with a thank you card that I designed to show his appreciation. The thank you card read; A special gift for you. It's my pleasure to be able to send you this lovely live palm tree as a gift of appreciation. "I hope you will enjoy it. It's just one way for me to say thank you for your continued efforts.

This plant reminds me of the way you nurture your business and help it develop and flourish. As you watch it grow, I hope, it will be a daily reminder to you of your potential for unlimited growth. With your proper care, your business can mature and grow to reach the heights you've dreamed of. You can achieve whatever you desire, because you're a special kind of person, and nothing is impossible." Thank you, signed by the president.

The little palm tree was overwhelmingly successful and the beginning of the "New Spirit of Avon." The president received thousands of phone calls, and thank you cards from the sales team thanking him for "caring." I followed up this program with the "Nu-Era of Achievement" recognition program, and the "Anniversary Reward" program. Both of these programs were designed to recognize and award the top sales performers, and both of these incentive programs would help increase net sales by having a planned motivational program that would immediately generate more sales. The secret potion that made these incentive programs work so phenomenally, and be so successful was one word, "motivation" which primarily focused on the following:

- Creativity: Individual recognition to uplift managers to new heights of efforts and self-esteem.- Timeless: Fine-Tuned: to specific individual goals within a defined time span.- Attainability: All managers would feel that they had an equal chance to win.- Morale Builder: Boost morale based on personal recognition.All of the new recognition programs were customized so there was something for everyone to strive toward achieving for their sales efforts, hard work and dedication. It was very important to openly and constantly recognize their sales performance so they would not feel undervalued and unappreciated.

After one year of introducing the new recognition and training programs, Avon's sales were beginning to show an increase. The "Big Sales Wheel" was beginning to move forward, and top senior management was thrilled with the sales results that the new programs had made in such a short period of time. It took a lot of hard work, but I was determined to make all the new programs be rewarding and successful. At the end of my first year at Corporate Headquarters, I was promoted to Manager of Sales Field Operations U.S. This was a big promotion with a lot more responsibilities. I would be responsible for all aspects of the new program called Opportunity Unlimited, and would be working with various Home Office Departments, Division and District Sales Managers to ensure a consistent line of communications, i.e., training, motivation, and recognition. My new office would be located on the 32nd floor, which is where all the top executive offices were located. It was a beautiful office, and had a fantastic view of Central Park East.I was thrilled to be moving up the "Corporate Ladder" to a top executive level position which was my goal. It was exciting to look back and see what I had achieved in such a short period of time. I was already looking forward to reaching my next goal of Vice President of Field Sales U.S., within the next year. I knew that if I was going to reach my next goal, I had my work cut out for me. I was excited, eager and ready to take on the challenge. I could see that my next career goal was definitely within reach.

◇

Chapter Twelve
Career Woman and Her Husband

After being back in New York, I continued to date the gentleman that I had been dating my last year in Cincinnati. Over the next year, he made many trips to visit and was beginning to like the life of the "Big Apple." He began talking about moving and getting married if his company would relocate him. "I was not looking for a husband." I was so career-oriented and getting married was not on my agenda even after being divorced for over fifteen years. Our relationship had gotten very serious, and I realized that we had definitely fallen in love, and I was truly enjoying spending time together. I was being very cautious because I did not want to make the same mistakes that led to a divorce in my first marriage of two young people that had totally different aspirations, goals and objectives that were not aligned.

As an ambitious career woman, it was important that I find a man with a strong ego, and a tremendous sense of self-esteem. I knew that a dual-career marriage could create a problem, and that coping with marriage responsibilities could be the single biggest problem that I would face as an executive, not because I was against marriage, but because I felt being married was a detriment to my career. "Being single made life a lot easier for me," simply because of business travel and evening business dinners. I knew that if I was going to have a successful marriage, I needed a man who would appreciate my zest for business life instead of feeling threatened by it, and he should be understanding, supportive, and an asset to my career. I found that the major problem in a dual-career marriage is that sometimes the man does not take his wife's career seriously. I knew that it would be hard to successfully merge a career and marriage unless I had a supportive husband who would take my career as seriously as his. The one thing that I knew for sure, was that he could not be a male chauvinist, because it would be hard to peacefully cohabitate with a person that is intrinsically opposed to the lifestyle that I had chosen. He could not be threatened by my success, and must be proud of me even if I made more money. He should see my career as a reflection of his good judgement in picking me as a partner, and consider himself lucky to be paired with an ambitious, and successful woman.

The day came when he asked me to marry him. I was very nervous and a little bit afraid even though he possessed most of the qualities that were important to me in a marriage relationship. I knew that he truly loved me. I accepted his proposal based on him having a job in New York City before moving and before we got married. He asked his company to relocate him to New York City because he wanted to get married. They told him that at that time they had no positions open at his level in the New York office. A few weeks later he invited me to fly out to Cincinnati to attend a big corporate executive dinner that a lot of the key executives from the Corporate Headquarters in Detroit would be attending. I flew out to Cincinnati to attend the business function, where I had an opportunity to meet most of the key executives from the corporate office. I knew that they were sizing me up with all the questions they were asking, but what they failed to realize is that I was in a top executive managerial position;

therefore, I knew how to professionally handle business corporate executives. The next day, I flew back to NYC, and one day later, I got a call from my future husband telling me that he had received a call from his corporate office, and they had found a position for him and would relocate him because they did not want to lose him as an employee. My secretary said when she looked at my face, while I was talking to him on the phone, she thought that I was going to faint after hearing the news. It all seemed to happen so fast. I was excited, but a little bit nervous because he would officially be relocating to New York City in a few weeks.

After over two years of dating, we decided to make the big move and get married. This was a second marriage for both of us. We decided to have a small wedding with my daughter, son and a few friends. After the wedding ceremony, we had dinner at "Windows on the World" restaurant which was located at the top of the World Trade Center it was wonderful. The next day we had a small get-together for family and friends at our condominium. We then took one week off from work to spend our honeymoon in Montego Bay, Jamaica where we enjoyed the white sandy beaches and the blue waters of the Caribbean Sea before buckling back down to work. We both knew that our only chance for a successful dual-career marriage would be through compromise and communication if it was to work. We definitely could not be competitive with each other, and hopefully, we would find companionship, comfort, love and security as a team, "Isn't that what marriage is all about?"

Life after marriage was great. We spent as much time as possible doing fun things together especially on weekends. One weekend we decided to go to the New York Boat Show where we saw a new twenty-seven-foot Sea Ray Sundancer, and immediately fell in love with it. We both loved boating, and we decided to purchase the boat which slept four people, a small kitchen galley, and a bathroom with a shower. We rented a boat slip at a mariner in Lindenhurst Long Island, New York where we spent the summers cruising the Great South Bay over to Fire Island National Seashore and out to Montauk Point, Long Island. We truly had some great times, and met a lot of really nice boating people.

At this point in our lives, we were both making great career accomplishments which kept us very busy during the week. My primary focus was to work on what I called, "People Power," because whatever marketing directions I was going to take or whatever goals and objectives were established would need to be accomplished through the efforts of the sales management team who would have a direct or indirect impact on sales. I knew that the new motivational programs that focused on the power of the sales management team would offer each of them long and short-term incentives that would effectively influence, motivate and recognize all top sales performers. These new motivational programs would uplift them to new heights of effort and self-esteem, and reward those who could perform, and change sluggishness into enthusiasm and excitement. The motivational/recognition programs coupled with training were beginning to show a tremendous change in morale and sales increases for the company. It would give each manager a voice to provide both positive and constructive feedback, and a chance to be open and share their honest thoughts. The more they felt like an important part of the team, the more likely they were to continue to offer their insight and ideas, which would help improve the company sales, and make the managers feel valued and respected.

I shared with you earlier that my career goals and aspirations were to be a trailblazer for women by breaking through the "glass ceiling" which was a barrier to prevent women from rising to higher corporate executive levels especially in sales which was a male-dominated field. It was truly a form of discrimination against women, I wanted to strive to make things easier for women who would follow, especially Black women. With a lot of grit and determination, I was able to achieve my business career goals with three different companies, Beech-Nut Corporation,

Burlington Industries and Avon Products, where I was the first woman of any color to be hired in sales, and in a sales management position. I am very proud to know that I helped to break down the color barrier for Black Models in the fashion world.

In order for me to be a pacesetter in a male-dominated field, I had to believe in myself and work toward achieving my goals in order to bring a real change in the corporate work environment. There were three factors that I believe influenced my success. They were visualization, belief and action. My long-term ultimate goal was to one day use all that I had learned in the corporate world and become an entrepreneur owning my own business working for myself. I had spent years, learning all I could about business, i.e., sales, marketing and advertising. Over the years I had been very successful in managing large corporate departments with multi-million dollars in sales.

I begin to think into the future about owning my own business, I had already created a unique name, obtained a business license, and opened a business bank account. The name that I had chosen was Classic Designs, Ltd. which was a unique name that would show the type and uniqueness of the business with emphasis on high-end gifts, and home decorative accessories that I wanted to offer my customers, and it would be an easy name for customers to remember. I had always known that I wanted to feature gifts, and home decorative accessories because I have an innate ability to know how to accessorize, and make things look beautiful in the home.

The first thing I needed to do was to identify if this was the right kind of business for me. I would need to focus on my objectives, strategies and action plan if I was going to achieve my entrepreneur goal. I knew that for me to be successful in my own business, it was important that I be self-motivated, a risk taker, have flexibility, passion, and know that the products that I wanted to offer would fit into the marketplace. I needed to know who would buy the products, and the size of the target market to determine if this type of business, and products were needed. I asked myself, where do I start my research? I decided to start by attending the largest Gifts and Home Decorative wholesale trade show in America. This show is held twice a year at the Jacob Javits Convention Center in New York City for retailers and specialty wholesale buyers. This is where manufacturers are showcasing their very best products for the home, lifestyle, and gifts. The show usually draws over 45,000 attendees from all 50 states and 80 plus countries with over 2,500 suppliers who are exhibiting and showcasing their very best line of products from around the world. This is where you as a retail buyer can find innovative home decorative designs, and trend-setting gifts. This show is a must attend event for retail buyers. It is where you have an opportunity to find your next bestseller, and develop a business relationship with the manufacturers.

We spent two days at the Trade Show visiting with most of the manufacturers. It was exciting to see so many new innovated products that would definitely have great potential for the type of business that I had interest in pursuing. We left the show with a lot of brochures and business cards. Weeks later, I decided to test the market by running a classified ad in the *New York Times* newspaper. But first, I needed to get a business account set up with Visa and Mastercard so I would be able to accept credits cards. At that time brass decorative items for the home were very fashionable. At the Trade Show I saw a beautiful pair of adorable brass deer that were the most charming pair of deer that I had ever seen. I knew that they would make an absolute perfect gift for the Christmas Holidays, I immediately made contact with the manufacturer to purchase some of the brass deer. Then, I placed a classified ad in October in the *New York Times* Sunday Shopping Mart Magazine section to test the market. It was an eye-catching adorable classified ad with a picture of the beautiful pair of brass deer, stating that they would be an absolute must for the Christmas Holidays, and truly a decorative beauty.My husband was skeptical that people would not order a product that was featured in a classified ad in a newspaper, and pay by credit card. Two days after the ad ran in Sunday's newspaper, we stopped by the post office to pick up the mail. The response was amazing, and we were thrilled to find so many mail baskets filled with orders. It was overwhelming and hard to believe how many orders we had received after only two days. After working on our regular jobs during the day, we would pack and ship orders in the evenings, and on weekends, it took us weeks to process all the orders. The timing was right because it was the beginning of a mail-order era. In the early 1980s, there were only a few mail-order catalogs, i.e., JC Penney's, Sears Roebuck, and Spiegel. Ordering things by mail was rare at that time, and credit cards were just beginning to become popular.

As a result of the classified ad being so successful, I quickly decided to put together a four-colored brochure featuring sixteen beautiful decorative brass items for holiday gift ideas, and each item was designed to capture the Christmas Holiday Season. The cover of the brochure was beautiful, and it read, "Christmas Magic in Brass." Where Classic Designs gifts are always welcomed for their originality and their unusual appeal. I mailed the Christmas brochure to over 5,000 potential customers in the state of New York, to a list of names and addresses that I had purchased from American Express. The response to the Christmas brochure was overwhelming, and we had a tough time packaging and shipping out all of the orders before Christmas. Wow, I learned from this experience that believing, being creative, and a little hard work can get you great sales results. The most important thing I learned was that there was a market for the type of gifts, and home decorative products that I wanted to feature in my entrepreneur business.

Chapter Thirteen
The Great Dual-Career Divide

Our marriage life was fantastic. We were truly in love, and enjoyed spending time with each other. My husband was enjoying the New York lifestyle. We knew that sharing our lives with another person could be challenging, and if our marriage was going to work, and we were going to be truly happy, and have a successful marriage, it would take commitment, love, respect, and trust. It was important that we talk to each other regularly, and always be open and honest about our feelings. At this point in our lives, we were both having great career successes, making outstanding accomplishments, and we both were focused on advancing our careers, and our own professional endeavors. We knew that a long-term career with a company could require relocation, which could create unique challenges and opportunities for us as a dual-career couple. Then the day came, when we had to face our first major dual-career transition as a couple, and to figure out how we could navigate through this major life changing event together, because this was a big relocation career opportunity for one of us.

My husband had called my office to tell me, that he had been offered a big promotion with a big salary increase. He was being promoted to Assistant Western Regional Sales Manager, and he would be covering all of the West Coast States, including Alaska and Hawaii, and his new office would be located in California. He was excited. He would be the first Black person with his company to be promoted to this management level. This was an outstanding promotion, and it came with a big salary increase, making it just too significant to refuse. The promotion did create a relocation problem that we knew one day we would have to face head-on. We were both very excited about his promotion. However, the big issue was, what does this move do to my career? It was not just what does this relocation mean for his career, but what does it mean for us. Relocating can often be great for your personal and professional development, "but it can be a risk leaping into the unknown." When one person must relocate to move up the corporate ladder, the other person has a difficult choice to make. These circumstances can lead to important questions, specifically about relocation, "whose career takes priority?" When you are in a dual-career marriage deciding whose career takes precedence, it was not an easy choice to make because it involved us making a decision that we needed to consider very carefully. We needed to ask ourselves, would this relocation bring us greater opportunities as a whole, and could we approach this new opportunity with a sense of adventure and openness? Generally, when one person must relocate to move up the corporate ladder, the other person has a difficult choice to make, whose career would lead and whose would follow? These circumstances can to an important question about relocation, whose career takes priority? How can we avoid having one person feeling like their career was being left behind? We asked ourselves, should we approach this new career opportunity with a sense of being creative and flexible in making our decision on what would be best for both of us. This was challenging, and the decision needed to be made jointly.

It was a time in my life when I was excited, happy and sad. I asked myself, what happens to my career? The career that I had worked so hard to achieve, and had been able to reach the level of being an Executive Sales Manager for three major Fortune 500 Companies. I had received two promotions within two years and I believed that I was within six to twelve months of reaching my next big promotion just based on the outstanding sales results of the new innovative incentive/recognition programs that I had created, developed and introduced to the sales field team. I felt that I was right on target for reaching my next promotion. I was so close, "I could see the rainbow at the end of the tunnel." I kept asking myself, was I willing to compromise my career? I had a long conversation with my mother regarding this situation. She asked me, if I truly loved my husband? I told her, yes, she said that nothing says love like packing up your life, and starting over in a new city with the person you love. My mother was very wise and had always given me good sound advice, and I truly trust her judgement. I prayed every day asking God to guide me through this promotion/relocation challenge. I asked him to help me make the right decision that would be best for both of us, especially for myself, so that later in life, I would not look back having regrets, and feeling like I had sacrificed my career that I had worked so hard to achieve. This was the first time in my life that I had to consider another person in making a career decision. I kept asking myself, how do I make this decision without being selfish? My husband's company knew that we had a dual-career marriage, therefore, they had given him two weeks to decide if he wanted to accept the promotion. I had been to California many times to visit, but never thought of living there. I loved living on the East Coast especially in New York City, and this is where my company's corporate headquarters was located, and my future career advancements could be made.

After many discussions regarding the potential new changes in our lives, we ultimately made our decision as to what would be best for us as a couple rather than what was best for either of us alone, and whose career would take precedence without the thought of whose career was more important. It was not an easy decision to make, it placed a lot of stress on me personally. I tried to look at it as a greater potential to increase opportunities, and further enhancement of our lifestyle. Since nobody was dependent, diverse relocation opportunities could open up for each of us. We found that talking and being open and honest about what we were feeling was our best way to keep our marriage healthy and successful. One of the greatest things about being a dual-career couple is that you get to share a common goal, and work harmoniously together to reach the goal effectively, giving each person a greater sense that the accomplishment was achieved by both.

Fortunately for me, my company had a large branch office in the same area where my spouse was being relocated. Therefore, requesting a transfer was a practical solution. The transfer would allow me not to lose my seniority or start over in terms of fringe benefits. Sometimes a new job and relocating can be life changing, and it can be a nerve-wracking endeavor. It's common for a person to feel a flood of emotions, excitement, nervousness, regret and even panic. Relocating can be one of the most stressful experiences a person can face. I know, because this would be my fifth business career relocation. That's why it was worth us taking time to determine if this relocation was the best for both of us. I asked myself how do I explain my dilemma? Especially when it came to making a choice between a difficult situation and a problem. "I kept asking myself was I crazy, or was I just in love?"

After we finally made our decision, my husband told his company that he would accept the promotion/relocation. It was now time for me to request a transfer/relocation package from my company for personal reasons. But before setting up the appointment, I made sure that my transfer request was a well thought out proposal. One that I could carefully and respectfully, present to the Vice President. I knew that I had proven my value and was valuable to the company. I was hoping that they would be willing to find a sales management position for me at the Branch Office in Pasadena. I assured the Vice President that I would do everything I could to ensure a smooth transition in order for the new sales manager to be able to hit the ground running with the current team being up to speed before leaving. He was shocked by the news, and told me that he would need to discuss this with the President of the company. He assured me that they would get back to me as soon as possible.

A couple of days later, I had an appointment to meet with the President. As a woman, the President had become as close to being my mentor as you could get during those times in a corporate environment. He was always encouraging and supportive of all the new creative incentive ideas and programs that I presented to help motivate, recognize and bring back that Avon "caring" feeling among the Sales Field Management team. Some of corporate management use to say that the President thought, "I could walk on water," especially after the introduction of some successful programs that had made a major impact on morale and sales.

During the meeting, the President asked me if relocating was what I wanted to do? I shared with him that I had given it a lot of thought, and because I was in a dual-career marriage, I had decided that it was the best thing to do for both of us as a team. He shared with me that my career with Avon was long-term with upper mobility, and he thanked me for my time and hard work, and said that losing me on his team would definitely be a company loss. He told me that he had approved the transfer/relocation request for me to transfer to the Pasadena Branch Office as a Field Sales Manager. Where I would be responsible for twenty-four District Sales Managers, and a large territory that covered all of Riverside, San Bernardino, part of Los Angeles, and Orange counties. He said that I would attain my current corporate salary, which was higher than the Pasadena Branch salaries, and my salary would continue to be paid through the corporate office in New York City. He assured me that I would be keeping all of my fringe benefits, and that the company would cover all relocation expenses. He asked me, if I would stay in my current position in New York for two months to finish up some of the new motivation/recognition programs that I had introduced to the sales field that were just beginning to show sales results. I thanked and assured him that I would do all I could to help make the transition as smooth as possible.

Our careers and relocation decisions had been made, and we were both overwhelmed with everything that needed to be done over the next few months. We began by making a few trips to California to look for a home near our new places of employment. After a few trips, we found an area that we fell in love with, and decided to build a new home, since we had time before making our final relocation move. We both kept very busy trying to tie loose ends together especially at work. The time went faster than I thought, and before I realized it was time to say goodbye to the city and job that I loved. My department and other coworkers gave me a big elaborate surprise going away party. The food and drinks were outstanding, and there were a lot of gifts from where else but Tiffany's. One of the gifts, I cherish, and still have on display in my home is a beautiful 14K gold Tiffany clock that is engraved with the following message "With love from all your N.Y. Avon Friends."

California here we come! We were moving up the executive corporate ladder, and looking forward to our new life, and endless possibilities. Relocating can be very difficult and challenging, but we managed to get everything done on the East and West Coasts. We sold our condominiums in New York, and had a new home built in Diamond Bar, California, and contracted with a moving company to move our car, boat and all our household and personal items. We made arrangements for temporary housing until our new home was built. This relocation for both of us turned out to be very expensive, but everything was completely covered by both of our companies' relocation packages. Once we got relocated, we begin to do the things that we both truly enjoyed which was boating, and we were able to get a boat slip at the picturesque Dana Point Harbor which is a prime waterfront marina located on the Pacific Ocean in Orange County. We spent many weekends out on our boat enjoying many activities like boating up and down the Pacific Coast, water sporting, whale watching, shopping and dining with family and friends. It seemed like the good times were always rolling at the Marina, with so many events, and activities.

Starting my new position in California came with a flood of emotions, and the beginning of a new chapter in my life. As I settled into the position, I tried to treat each day as a new learning opportunity. My primary focus was being able to execute the responsibilities of the new job, then seek out what needed to be done, and then go do it. I wanted to make the best first impression, and be the kind of person who lived up to that impression. I wanted to see each day as an opportunity where I could use my God-given talent, and execute the responsibilities of the new position. The new division that I had been assigned covered four counties, Riverside, San Bernardino, part of Los Angeles, and Orange. San Bernardino County is the largest county in the state of California. These four counties accounted for over $20 million in annual sales revenue. There were no Blacks among the twenty-four District Sales Managers, and very few Blacks among the 5,000 Sales Representatives, and less than 10 percent of the population in the division was Black. The division covered some beautiful areas, Palm Springs, the mountains, and the desert where you didn't find a large Black population. My primary responsibility was managing, training and developing the District Sales Managers to help them grow and develop, and be able to train and motivate the Sales Representatives. I spent about 70 percent of my time traveling, and about 30 percent in the office taking care of all the administrative work, and attending staff meetings. I used a lot of the same training and motivational programs that I had used in training and motivating the Sales Manager team in Cincinnati. These programs had been overwhelmingly successful, and had helped to generate outstanding sales results. During the next few years, I spent a lot of time working with the management team to get them to the level of showing personal development and sales growth. One of the greatest things about living in Southern California is the weather, it is always beautiful, which gave me an opportunity to spend more time working in the field with each manager, which helped the districts, and the division to have some outstanding sales increases.

After becoming adjusted to the new position and environment, I began to have visualizations of when I wanted to move from working for an employer to being an entrepreneur business owner. I thought about it every day, and I knew that I would not stop thinking about it until I did it, and that would only happen when I made a conscious decision to make it happen. I began to focus on the four factors that could influence my entrepreneurial success; visualization, belief, action, and being willing to take a risk, I had always enjoyed the elements of being a risk taker, and was always willing to gamble on myself. However, being an entrepreneur starting your own business would be playing where the stakes were high, and in order to start my business, I would need financial backing, and an extraordinary amount of courage, and good luck. Statistics show that four out of five new businesses fail due to being undercapitalized. There's a saying, "You need money to make money," and this certainly is true when starting a business. I knew there was one critical step I needed to take to be successful, and that was to believe, and see myself as a successful business owner.

Yes, I wanted to start my own business, but I kept asking myself where do I start? I knew that being an entrepreneur could be an exciting and liberating endeavor, and extremely challenging. It could have benefits, and give me an opportunity to take a risk, in being able to create something from nothing with endless possibilities. There was nothing that would make me work harder and smarter than owning my own business, which would give me motivation and discipline to be the hardest-working version of myself. In every decision that I have had to make, I've always asked God to help me make the right decision for myself and everyone involved. "Then I would leap out on faith." Knowing that God was my safety net, I have always believed that there is a path that has been designed for each person, and I truly believed that I had found mine, which was to be the owner of Classic Design, Ltd. a high-end gifts and home decorative accessories business. I chose the name Classic Designs Ltd., because it was a distinctive business name that showed uniqueness, and my type of business. While we were living in New York, I had an opportunity to do some advertising to test the market to see if there was a demand for the type of products that I want to sell. The sales results were overwhelming, which assured me that there was a demand, and a target group of people that were interested in purchasing the products that I planned to sell.

After giving it a lot of consideration, I decided to start the process by first opening a business bank account, and developing a business plan that would need to be well organized if I wanted to succeed. I applied for a DBA "Doing Business As" license for California, and a Federal & State Employer Identification Number (EIN), which is a federal ID that allows you to hire employees to work, and ensures that the business collects payroll taxes. The business plan would need to show how I would pay taxes and employees. It was critical that I have an outstanding business plan to present to the banks, and it would help me to gain clarity, focus and confidence. My ultimate goal was to build a lifestyle business; therefore, it was important that I have a detailed understanding of my personal finances before seeking outside financial funding for the business. As I began to work on the business plan, I kept my focus on believing that, "If I believed in my business, others would too."

I continued to work on my job during the day, and my business plan at night, and on weekends. Once I completed the business plan, I had an opportunity to present it to a few banks, and the Small Business Administration. They all agreed that my business plan and business career background was very impressive, but they were unable at that time to make a small business loan to first-time business owners. They each tried to assure me that they would be very interested if I needed a loan after getting my store open, or to open a second store. I did finally find a bank that was willing to make me a small business loan simply because they felt confident that if I followed my business action plan, I would be successful. With the bank business loan, and my own resources, I decided that it was now time to move forward and open my retail store.

My next move was to find the right location near where I lived. My timing was perfect. I checked around and learned that there was going to be a vacant storefront in the Diamond Bar Ranch Shopping Center which was a very prominent shopping center located in Diamond Bar where I lived. Diamond Bar is a beautiful upper middle-class community with the average household income being over $100,000 per year which would give me the type of clientele that I needed to purchase the type of high-end products that I wanted to sell. The shopping center had excellent exposure to two major freeways, and there were two great restaurants on the premises that had outstanding food, and they were always busy for lunch and dinner. The vacant storefront that was going to be available was located right in the middle of the shopping center, and was anchored between the two very popular restaurants. This was a prime location, and it would provide a lot of foot traffic and fantastic exposure. I was overwhelmed knowing that I had an opportunity to lease a storefront building in the Diamond Bar Ranch Shopping Center.

PICTURE OF ME AT BEECH-NUT

◇

Chapter Fourteen
My Entrepreneurial Dream Business

At this point in my life, I was inspired to achieve my ultimate goal. I decided to put all my faith, trust and hope in God, and myself. Trusting in God that this would be a successful business venture. I had always wanted to own my own business, and I had been preparing for this day for a long time. I had taken every business course that I could while working at my corporate positions. Yet, it was hard to believe that I had reached the day where I had an opportunity to actually open my first retail store, Classic Designs, Ltd., a high-end gift and home decorative accessory business, that would be located in Diamond Bar, California. I would feature crystal, Llardo handmade and hand-painted porcelain figurines, Armani collectibles, Fitz and Floyd hand-painted dinnerware, specialty gifts, high-end home decorative accessories, and a bridal registry. The Fitz and Floyd beautiful hand-painted dinnerware, and the Llardo wedding figurines made the perfect wedding gift, and of course there would be beautiful free gift wrapping. After signing the lease, I had two months to get ready for the "Grand Opening." The first thing I needed to do was to resign from my current position with Avon Products, and wrap up all loose ends before leaving. Next was getting the store remodeled, and doing some massive advertising, and marketing for the Grand Opening. I needed to hire and train four sales people ensuring that they had product knowledge, and good customer service skills. For the Grand Opening, I would need a lot of inventory. I made arrangements to go to the gift shows in New York, and Los Angeles to purchase display racks, inventory, white glossy shopping bags with the name Classic Designs printed on each bag in gold, beautiful black and gold gift wrapping paper, gold ribbon and bows. It was an exciting time, and I was overwhelmed, but I was sure I would get everything done on schedule.

The "Grand Opening" finally arrived, and it was a magnificent and rewarding grand opening day. The special local advertising, and word of mouth paid off. It was amazing how many people came, and the incredible sales that were generated. "What a day," one that I will never forget. I had a special ribbon cutting ceremony which gave people a time to show up, and it suggested that something big and official was coming, and that was true, it was a new retail business. I planned a big opening day in order to spread the word about the new business, and I was giving a 20 percent discount on all items purchased, and there was a special drawing for a beautiful "Waterford Crystal Vase." The drawing was a way for me to get names and addresses so I could create a customer mailing list. Because there is nothing more important than repeat customers who are essential in keeping the business afloat, and nothing is more powerful than word of mouth advertising. I knew that providing good service to my customers was crucial if I wanted to gain their loyalty, and retain their business. The "Grand Opening" day turned into a grand opening week which created exceptional enthusiasm, and excitement within the community.

Starting a new business was a lot of hard work, and it definitely was not something that I could do overnight. It took a consistent growth effort that took a lot of time. But I knew that the time, effort and hard work would equal growth and money in the long run, and there was nothing that pushed me to work harder and smarter than the responsibility of owning my own business. I stayed focused on achieving my short and long-term goals by making sacrifices, working harder and longer hours for myself than for anyone else. Owning my own business was an exciting and liberating endeavor that was constantly presenting new challenges. It was tough but it had its benefits. The best part of owning my own business was introducing new innovative products to my customers, and having the ability to create something from nothing making the possibilities endless. It gave me a chance to create my own definition of success because "I literally owned my own business."

I worked very hard every day. The store was successful and was showing a small profit. I had a lot of new and repeat customers who loved shopping at the store because I always had new innovative unique products, and they truly enjoyed the personal shopping, home decorative assistance, and the outstanding customer service.

Two years after opening the first store, an executive from the Montclair, California Shopping Mall stopped by the store. He told me that he had lunch a couple days a week at the restaurant next door, and was very impressed with the quality, and appearance of the store. He asked me, if I would be interested in opening a store in the new upscale shopping mall that was being built in Montclair, I jumped at the opportunity to have a chance to build my second store. Which would be on the second floor, two doors down from the famous Nordstrom Department store, and it would be located at the top of the escalator making it a prime location for exposure, and a lot of foot traffic. He guaranteed me that there would be no other stores in the mall like my store. Needless to say, with this new opportunity, I was overly thrilled and nervous. I asked myself, am I ready to make this big move? Owning a store in a small shopping center is quite different than owning one in a large shopping mall, i.e.; things like being open seven days a week, longer hours, more employees, and more inventory. He said that I would be the only woman, or African American to own a retail business in the new shopping mall. This was happening so fast, and it was a little scary, but I had always been a risk taker and a pacesetter. I was ready to take on the challenge. However, this was big, and in order for me to accomplish this goal, I would definitely need some outside financing. I quickly updated my original business plan and made an appointment with the Small Business Administration. After the first meeting they were impressed with the sales results of my first store, and immediately approved a small business loan. With the business loan, my own resources, and three of my friends who believed in me and were willing to make a small investment, I was able to open the store in Montclair. There are no words that could ever express my thanks to each of my friends for believing in me. However, I would like to take this opportunity, to thank each of them from the bottom of my heart, and let them know that I will forever be thankful for having special friends like them. "You know who you are." Thank you!

Four months later the new shopping mall was ready to celebrate its Grand Opening, and so was Classic Designs. It was the longest four months of my life. There had been so much that had to be done. I was determined to have an electric fireplace mantle built in the store to feature and showcase home decorative items and artwork where it would be used to help customers learn how to display the items that they purchase for their home. With the help of the new sales associates, the store displays and setups were amazingly beautiful, and breathtaking. I hired a person to help me to design and set up the window displays which turned out to be amazing and showstopping. The outside of the store was painted white, and the name Classic Designs was in bold beautiful gold letters above the entrance doors which made the store feel inviting and interesting, and created a lot of foot traffic. There are no words that could ever express the excitement and joy of the Grand Opening. It was sensational, and we were over-whelmed with the number of customers and sales. I had all the sales associates working to help keep up with the flow of customers.

Both of the stores were being successful and generating sales. I had built a loyal customer base of primarily women. I wanted to find a way to attract more men customers... I put together a personal shopping program for Classic Designs to help men remember those special dates in their life, i.e., birthdays, anniversaries, Mother's Day, Valentine's Day and other special holidays. This special program would help men to remember those dates, and assist them in selecting the perfect gift for that special person in their life. Each gift purchased would be beautifully gift wrapped, and they could take it with them, or pick it up at a later date. This special program was named "Just for the Gentlemen," and it was held on the first Tuesday of each month at 6:30 p.m. Champagne and hors d'oeuvres were served, and we offered a 20 percent discount on any purchase made that evening. The purpose of this function was to create a file for each of our male customers, and keep the information on file of the special people in their life. We would give them a call about a week before the special date to remind them of the upcoming important day, and make some suggestions as to what that person might like based on what information they had given us about that person. I had trained all the sales associates on how to work with each male customer, and what questions to ask about the person they were buying for in order to ensure that the perfect gift was selected. The feedback from wives after they had received a gift was amazing, they could not believe some of the beautiful gifts that they received from their husband, and often came to the store to see where it had been purchased. They would say that their husband had never given them such a beautiful gift, and especially one that they really loved. This turned out to be exceptionally successful, and I was able to create a lot of loyal male customers, and the store became their place to shop for those special occasions either in person or by phone.

Mother's Day, Christmas and the Bridal Registry were, without a doubt, the bustling times of the year. The Christmas season was always exciting and beautiful, and it was a great time to sell the type of products that we sold. Sales during the Christmas holiday season were phenomenal and made up a large portion of the annual sales. It was my favorite time of the year. The opening of the Christmas holiday season officially started the day after Thanksgiving, and both stores were beautifully decorated and they made you feel like you were in a "Christmas Wonderland." Both stores were exceptionally beautiful, and had Christmas music playing throughout during the holidays. To up the elegance, and be unique during the Christmas season all sales associates wore black tuxedos with red or green bow ties and cummerbund starting Thanksgiving Day up to Christmas Eve. On opening day for the Christmas holidays, we would have people waiting in line for the stores to open, where they were greeted by Santa Claus who welcomed each customer, and gave them a gift to wish them and their family a Merry Christmas from Classic Designs. Throughout the day, we served hot apple cider and gingerbread cookies which was always a favorite treat for the customers.

All Christmas gifts purchased were beautifully wrapped in red gift paper with gold ribbon and bows, and the Classic Designs gold seal was placed on every package, and then put in a beautiful glossy white shopping bag with the name Classic Designs printed in gold. If needed, we would deliver the packages to their car. After a few years, a lot of my loyal customers would bring in a list of names of people that were on their Christmas list, and leave it up to me to select a gift for each of them. On Christmas Eve they would pick up their beautifully wrapped Christmas gifts that I had selected for the people on their Christmas shopping list, not knowing what they had purchased for each person. "That's called trust." After Christmas a lot of people that received a gift from the store would stop by the store just to see where it was purchased. It was exciting to know that we had made a great gift selection, and gained another happy customer. During the Christmas holidays my spouse and my daughter would work part-time to help keep the flow of customers moving.

Over the next few years, the business continued to grow. I had built a large loyal customer base of women and men. Needless to say, operating two stores seven days a week kept me extremely busy handling all the employee roles, and being the president down to the janitor. There was never a free moment. It was at this point that I decided it was time to hire a manager for each store to help with some of the daily responsibilities, and to give me more time to focus on buying new innovative products, and working on developing a mail-order catalog. The timing was perfect for starting up a mail-order business, because there were only a few businesses at that time that offered a mail-order catalog. As I looked into the future of the retail business, I could see that the mail-order business was going to be the thing of the future. I based this on the outstanding sales results that I had received from the product brochures that I had mailed out to test the market while living in New York.

Every month the mall had a contest to recognize the store with the most creative and unique window display. I am proud to say that Classic Designs' won the contest almost every month. Each month our window display featured a specific theme. The final display results were always remarkable, and a real true show stopper for customers passing by to stop in and take a look. The business was moving smoothly, and showing a continuous growth in sales which was right on target. I loved owning my own business and there was always something that I could do to make improvements.

Starting my own business and watching it grow was an incredible thrill, but it placed a tremendous demand on me. My life had little room for anything else, and sometimes the responsibilities were staggering. I know, because I speak from experience of owning and operating two stores for many years. It was magnificent to feel in control of your destiny, and make my efforts pay off for myself. In order for me to accomplish my mission, I had to be willing to sacrifice myself, because the business took all that I had to give, but the rewards outweighed the difficulties. Owning my own business required a lot of courage, and a strong sense of self-confidence. I knew that if I was going to score big in the retail business, I would have to be willing to take a calculated risk, and have the courage to gamble on the outcome. I knew that if I wanted to survive, I had to possess great internal strength and fortitude, which the harsh demands of everyday life required. One of my favorite sayings is, "When the going gets tough, the tough get going." I worked hard on staying focused, counting my blessings, and not my problems.

Marriage life was good, my spouse was busy working to enhance his career, and helping me at the stores on weekends and holidays. We both knew that for him to achieve his ultimate career goal of reaching the unclassified executive level that he would probably have to relocate at least one or two more times. Reaching the unclassified level was very important. Because that is the executive level where you have an unclassified salary, annual bonus, stock options, stock rewards and other fringe benefits, and it is the level that you want to reach before retirement. The day came when he was told that he was being promoted to Zone Manager in St. Louis, and would be responsible for the Mid-Western states. This time, we were mentally ready for this news, and quickly made what we thought was the best decision for our dual-career marriage. We had discussed relocation many times, and we both decided that he would accept the promotion and relocate to St. Louis, and that I would stay in California to manage the business. We knew that this arrangement would create a challenging long-distance relationship, and a lot of commuting across country. The long-distance relationship worked out for us, but it is not something that I would recommend because it takes a real toll on your marriage. People often say that difficult roads, often lead to beautiful destinations. I know from my own experience that change is hard at first, and it can be messy in the middle, but great at the end. It is those tough situations in life that help to build strong people. One thing that I know for sure is that, "Life is tough, but so am I." My primary goal at that particular time was to accept what was now, let go of what was, and to have faith in what could be.

◇

Chapter Fifteen
Starting All Over Again

Two years later, my spouse was promoted again. This time he was being relocated to Washington, D.C. as Zone Manager responsible for all of the East Coast states. This Zone was larger than the Zone in St. Louis with a lot more responsibilities. Yes, of course, I was excited about his promotion, it was being relocated that always presented a challenge. But at this point, I had learned that the best solution to conquering the "great dual-career divide," was to establish priorities if we expected our relationship to work, would need to share equal importance with our careers, and to realize that sometimes you have to give the relationship first priority. Our task was to find new resolutions, new terms of agreements, and new arrangements. We realized that our only chance for a successful dual-career marriage was through compromise and communication. Without this, underlying resentment and jealousy would erode our relationship until it was destroyed. We tried to avoid this with frank and honest communication, with a lot of giving on both sides. We tried to make unique agreements that would be practical for our individual situation.

With this great promotion, and relocation, we both decided that it would be best to sell the retail business in California, and that I would move back to the East Coast. I loved my retail business, it had been my ultimate business dream goal, and I loved my husband, and "I knew that he loved me." Once again to get advice, I turned to my mother. I will forever cherish her words of wisdom. She told me that "Happiness is not something that you postpone for the future; it's something you cherish for the present." Throughout my life, I had always been a warrior fighting many battles and wars, and I know that I am who I am through the grace of God, and that this was the time in my life when I needed to allow myself to tap into God's power. Because it was God that had given me confidence and hope, and it was "hope" that allowed me to always see the bright side of things, and it was "hope" that has given me joy by leaning on my faith and courage. In my heart, I knew that this too shall pass. Making the decision to sell the business was very hard, but as a team we had made the decision to relocate back to the East Coast. That meant selling the business which had never really crossed my mind. But if I was going to relocate back to the East Coast, I would need to sell the business, our home, and purchase a new home in Maryland.

I was certain that we would have no problem selling our home in Diamond Bar because it was located in a new desirable community, and interest rates were low. I had some experience in selling and buying a home, but no experience in selling a retail business. However, I felt comfortable that I would be able to sell the stores, because both stores had prime locations, especially the store in the Montclair Shopping Mall. Over the years there had been very few weeks that went past that someone was asking me about purchasing the business, or if I was interested in setting up a franchise. Both stores were showing a consistent month-over-month growth in sales, which made it a good time to sell. It was just finding the right buyer, and making sure that I received the true value of the business. I knew that it was important that I have a good agent that had proven expertise, and familiarity with my type of business to help find the right buyer, and to help determine the estimated asking price. Selling the business required having all financial statements, and bookkeeping records organized, so the potential buyer could fully understand the profits and losses (P&L) of the business. I had always used an accounting firm to help keep financial records, i.e.; inventory, daily sales, payroll and taxes. Therefore, I had all the financial information needed to help position the business for a potential buyer.

Once the stores were on the market for sale, there were a number of potential buyers. Some of them, I personally chose not to sell the business to. I finally decided to sell to someone that had stopped by the store many times inquiring about buying, or wanting to know if I was interested in setting up a franchise. I knew what my business was worth, so when working with potential buyers, I was able to remove my emotions, and be able to negotiate firmly and effectively, in order to get the sales price that the business was worth. After the business was sold it took about two months to officially finalize the sale. Once all the papers had been signed, I finally realized that it was my last day at the store. It was hard to say a final goodbye to my brainchild before heading off to a new adventure. Selling the business had been very emotional – even if it was what I had decided to do. It was difficult to turn off the connection that I felt, and had worked so hard to get off the ground. Selling the business had not been anywhere near the forefront of my brain. I tried to remind myself of all the objectives that I had achieved since opening the stores, and the simple fact that I had built something that someone else wanted to buy, and I had sold the business. I asked myself what's next? I begin to brainstorm my next entrepreneurial idea. One very important thing that I learned during this whole process was to accept what is, let go of what was, and to have faith in what will be.

We were on the move again. We sold the retail business, and our home in California, and purchased a new home in Maryland,

and made arrangements with the moving company to relocate our household and personal items to our new home. It was a crazy and busy time but everything was falling in place, and I was looking forward to new adventures on the East Coast. Once we had moved to Maryland, I decided to take a little time off to rest and think about what I wanted to do career-wise. I could have gotten a position with a large corporation in sales management, but I knew that we would probably only be in Maryland for a few years. Therefore, I decided not to get back into the corporate world or to open another retail business.

After living in Maryland for a few months, I noticed that the real estate business was booming and interest rates were low. I decided to get my real estate license for the state of Maryland, and worked with the Coldwell Banker real estate agency. My objective was to concentrate primarily on corporate relocations. As a real estate agent, I would help employees that were being relocated with selling their current home, and buying a new home in their new location. During that time, most of the larger corporations were constantly relocating their employees, and the employee would need to sell their current home, and buy a new home. Over the years, I had a lot of contacts that I had made with people that were working for major corporations. My corporate contact would call to let me know when someone was being promoted and relocated. I would then contact that person, and assist them in selling their current home, and buying a new home at their new location anywhere in the United States. These were guaranteed sales because the employees' relocation expenses were covered by their company's relocation package, and I would earn a six percent commission on the selling and buying of the employees' homes. This turned out to be an extremely lucrative business, that didn't require a lot of time. Over the next two years, I truly enjoyed working and living in Maryland. We took advantage of visiting all the surrounding states, and made many trips to Washington, D.C. and New York City where I had a lot of friends.

We were now entering into another phase of our lives, my spouse had been promoted to Western Regional Sales Manager, and was being relocated back to California where he would be responsible for the West Coast States, including Alaska and Hawaii. This was his ultimate career goal to reach the unclassified executive level where he would be able to take advantage of having an unclassified salary, stock bonuses, and all the other top executive fringe benefits. This is the level that an employee strives to achieve before retirement. It is at this level that the retirement benefits are fantastic. Needless to say, we were both thrilled about the promotion, and being relocated back to California where we would be near our children and grandchildren. With us having so many relocations over the years, I was beginning to dread the re-location process which can be very stressful, but it can have a lot of positives, and offer some fantastic new opportunities.

After relocating seven times over the years for career opportunities, this relocation was a breeze. I had a lot of experience in relocating, and knowing how to start all over again in a new city. Our home in Maryland sold quickly, and we had a new home built in Moorpark, California which is a beautiful area, and it was very close to my spouse's office, and our daughter's home. Of all the homes that we had lived in, the home in Moorpark was my favorite because it was built on a hill and had a fantastic view of the moun-tains. My spouse quickly adjusted to his new work environment, and was doing a lot of business traveling. I had always enjoyed working, therefore, I decided to continue my career in Real Estate, and to help keep my business skills sharp. I agreed to work with my son to help him build his communication, health and fitness business. This business turned out to be incredibly successful. We worked very hard and had some great mother and son times to-gether, ones that I will cherish forever. There is an old saving that I believe is true, i.e., "Son like mother, he is definitely a workaholic and success driven."

While living in Moorpark I decided to do some volunteer charity work in my spare time. My son was on the Board of Directors with Athlete & Entertainers for Kids (AEFK) which was a national nonprofit educational mentoring organization to bring Corporate America together with athletes and entertainers to help disadvantaged youth who lack positive role models and guidance. AEFK's goal was to encourage youth to remain in school, graduate, and seek educational opportunities. During that time, they were able to influence over 500,000 city-kids ages three to nineteen by exposing them to inspirational celebrities like basketball player Shaquille O'Neal who played for The Lakers, supermodel Kathy Ireland, and Tim Brown a Heisman Trophy Winner, and NFL football player with the Oakland Raiders. There were many famous celebrities that donated their time and money by having interaction with the kids, and I had an opportunity to meet and work directly with each of them for such a great cause. I have great memories of the faces on those kids when they had an opportunity to meet and spend time with one of the celebrities playing golf, or especially once a year when Universal Studios in Hollywood would close for "Shaq Attack Day," this function was named after Shaq. On that special day, we would bus in hundreds of inner city-kids to spend the day with Shaq O'Neal, and other celebrities. The cost of the food and all rides for the day was donated by celebrities and corporations. The kids had a great time, I really thought that Shaq had more fun than the kids.

During the time we lived in Maryland, we had given up boating and had gotten into motor-homing. Our very first motorhome was a thirty-four-foot Pace Arrow. After having the motorhome for a few years, we realized that we truly enjoyed this lifestyle and made a decision to move up to a forty-foot Country Coach Affinity which we loved. Once we were hooked into enjoying that lifestyle, we moved up to a forty-five-foot Country Coach Prevost, it was a beauty. It was a Class A motorhome that could sleep four people, had a full-size bathroom and shower, three flat-screen televisions, dishwasher, and washer and dryer combo. It definitely offered all the comforts of home with everything we needed for our motorhome adventures. It offered us the freedom on the open road, where we were able to chase the sun and take off whe-never we wanted. This is a dream of many people who want to have an opportunity to see North America which is loaded with beautiful, scenic, historic, and friendly destinations that can fill a lifetime of adventure with all the super convenience right from the comfort of your motorhome. With the California weather, we were able to enjoy the motorhome year-round. We decided to purchase two motorhome lots; Outdoor Resorts in LaQuinta that we could use during the fall/winter months, and Big Bear Shores which was on the lake Big Bear that we could use during the summer months. We had a lot of motorhome friends, and had an opportunity to travel to forty-eight states and Canada. During those years, we had a group of friends that bonded, and we had some great times traveling and partying together. We enjoyed trav-eling because it is an adventure you can take to live the life of your dreams, simply by creating memories and leaving footprints. I believe that life begins at the end of your comfort zone, and that's why I have done things totally out of my comfort zone, i.e., white water rafting in Oregon, parasailing in Cancun, Mexico, zip lining in Cabo, Mexico, landing on the top of a glacier in a helicopter in Alaska, and hot air ballooning in Albuquerque, New Mexico. I have learned over the years that the biggest adventure you can ever take is to live the life of your dreams. "My goal is to die with a lot of memories not dreams."

Our lives were going great, and we were truly enjoying living and working in California, which gave us a chance to spend a lot of time with our two beautiful grandchildren. We had never been in the same location for seven years, so it had been wonderful not having to relocate and start all over in a different part of the country. We had both worked for many years in the corporate environment, and we had planned, and prepared for early retire-ment, ensuring that we would have enough retirement benefits, to live the lifestyle that we had become accustomed to, and we wanted to be able to do a lot of traveling to see the world.

Chapter Sixteen
My Retirement Career

In our eighth year, once again we were faced with my spouse being offered a position at the company's headquarters in Detroit, Michigan. We were hoping that he would be at the California office for at least two more years, since we were planning to take early retirement. We discussed the pros and cons of another relocation, and decided not to accept the new position in Detroit. Simply because, we had decided that we wanted to retire in California, therefore, we did not want to be in Detroit where we would have to relocate ourselves back to California. When my spouse met with his manager, he expressed his appreciation for the promotion/relocation, and that he was grateful that they saw potential in him. He affirmed his commitment and loyalty to the company and clearly explained that it was not the right time or right fit for us to relocate to Detroit at this time in our lives. Simply because we were thinking about taking early retirement within the next two years, after being with the company for over thirty-five years. A few months later they offered him an early retirement severance package that included what's known as bridging. This is where supplemental income has been designed to bridge the gap between early retirement, and this is where having an unclassified executive salary, and all the other fringe benefits really kicked in. We were thrilled with the retirement package that they offered. One thing that I have learned, is that the key to being happy is knowing you have the power to choose what to accept, when to let go, and by having a lot of faith in what will be. When I look back over my life, I know that every day, and every adventure was a learning opportunity

After forty years of working, we both had retired and were spending a lot of time traveling around the world. We had traveled extensively with our careers, and were really excited about seeing the world on our own schedule. We have had an opportunity to travel all over the United States, and Canada in our motorhome. We enjoy going on cruises, and have taken thirty cruises to places like Tahiti, France, Italy, Spain, Greece, Turkey, England, and all over the Caribbean, Bahamas, Bermuda, Mexico, Alaska, Hawaii and Canada. We've had an opportunity to travel to Africa, Austria, China, Germany, Ireland, and Scotland. Life has been good, and we have truly been blessed.

After retiring, we decided that we wanted to retire in Palm Desert, California, and the first thing we needed to do was to downsize from a two-story 4,000 square foot home, to something smaller on one level with no stairs. We decided to sell our home in Moorpark, and have a smaller one-story home built in LaQuinta, which is often referred to as the desert. When building our home, I had all the upgrades that I ever wanted put in the home, I had no intentions of ever moving again during my lifetime, and that's why I called that home "my take me to glory home." After a few years of being retired and traveling, I realized how much I missed the excitement and challenges that you have to face each day when you are working, I really missed that work environment, simply because I loved the positions that I had in sales and sales management for three major corporations. What I loved most about sales was that you are always competing with yourself, and this was a real motivator for me knowing that my sales results were based on my own performance.

I decided to get a part-time sales position with JW Marriott as a marketing sales coordinator selling time shares for their new development in Palm Desert. The JW Marriott was a beautiful place to work, and each day I met people from all over the world. I only worked five hours, two or three days a week, no weekends. Over the years I had developed outstanding selling skills; therefore, I quickly became their top marketing sales coordinator. After six months, I had sold $1,232,560 which qualified me to be inducted into the Sapphire Club which was the Million Dollar Club. I received recognition and a beautiful engraved trophy. My sales performance ranked me as the No.1 marketing sales coordinator. Over the next six years, my sales were over $1 million each year, and each quarter, and year-end I received a lot of awards and special recognition. The company offered me a training position at their Corporate Office in Florida, where I would have the responsibility of developing and conducting training seminars for the company's sales coordinators worldwide. I turned down the job offer because I had retired and was not looking to take on another full-time career which would involve relocation, or a lot of traveling. However, I did agree to develop a sales training program, and do some training seminars for the marketing sales coordinators locally to help boost our team's sales. With the salary, bonuses, stock, and being able to stay at any Marriott hotel or resort anywhere in the world was simply outstanding. It was a great company and a beautiful place to work, and I truly enjoyed working there.

◇

Chapter Seventeen
Caring for My Mom

After working for the JW Marriott part-time for six years, I found myself now faced with how to best care for my aging parents, who lived in Arkansas. My mother had just been diagnosed with Alzheimer's, and my dad had heart problems. I was faced with making a decision on what to do. I asked myself, do I move my mother to California to live with us, or do I uproot my life and move there to care for her, or should I try to manage things from long distance, or just put her in a skilled nursing home? None of these choices were going to be an easy decision to make. Initially, we decided to move her out to California to live with us. However, she was unhappy not being in her own familiar surroundings, I then decided to go to Arkansas to see if I could find a live-in caregiver. However, after interviewing a few people, I quickly realized that was not going to work out to my satisfaction especially with me being so far away. I decided that I wanted to take care of her which meant uprooting and moving to Arkansas. I did not feel obligated to move to care for her, but I had always had a great relationship with my mother, and my parents had been so good to me, I asked myself, "How could I leave her there by herself?" After discussing the pros and cons with my spouse, we decided to move to Arkansas which meant selling my "Take me to Glory Home" in California. I notified the Marriott of my decision to care for my mother, and they gave me a year's leave of absence. Moving to Arkansas to care for my mother was a big step, but it was one that I wanted to take. We sold our retirement home in California, and cleared off two acres of land in Arkansas, and built a home on land that I had inherited from my great-grandfather who had purchased the land in 1894. After our home was built, I moved my mother in to live with us. After being in Arkansas for one year taking care of my mother, I found myself taking care of my dad, and my aunt who lived across the road. My dad and mom had been divorced for years, and he lived about sixty miles from where she lived, and he was having severe heart problems. I wanted to help them to live out their independence, a familiar lifestyle, and most importantly, allow them to stay home as long as possible. I wanted to create a positive quality of life for them, especially for my mother who was suffering from Alzheimer's. This disease has to be the worst, just seeing a person losing all of their memories. I quickly realized that in order for me to understand this complicated disease, that I needed to attend some seminars on Dementia and Alzheimer's in order to learn how to take care of her. These seminars helped me to learn how to understand and communicate with her daily in a positive manner, and how to set a positive mood, in order to limit distractions and ease her frustration. I tried to always respond to her with a soft voice tone in order to add reassurance, and help reduce her anxiety and confusion. Most people underestimate the time it takes to be an Alzheimer's caregiver, and the amount of stress that is placed on the caregiver daily. Most days, I was totally overwhelmed and sometimes not knowing for sure exactly what was needed to be done. There were many days that caring for three elderly people was extremely stressful, and it left little or no time for me to have a personal life. I prayed daily, and asked God to give me courage and strength.

I was able to help care for my dad for three years before he passed at age ninety-four, then a few months later my aunt at age eighty-five, and two years later my mother at age ninety-three. I truly miss them. It was a daily challenge, but I am so happy that I was able to be there to add a little enjoyment for each of them during the last few years of their lives. I love this special saying, "If your parents cared for you, care for them, because one day you will be older, and unable to care for yourself." Ask yourself this question, who will care for me when I am older? I realize that not everything that I have done in life has pleased everybody, but I asked myself whose life am I living, theirs or mine?

After my mother passed, I found myself bored after having been so busy every day taking care of elderly parents and aunt. I began to think about what I had learned as a caregiver, and how could I use this knowledge to help other aging seniors especially the ones that were turning age sixty-five to understand how the Medicare system works. Over the years taking my parents to the doctors and hospital, I had met so many seniors who had made bad medical insurance decisions because of a lack of knowledge, and now found themselves in a situation where they were unable to make changes to their Medicare insurance; therefore, limiting themselves to be able to seek out the best professional medical doctors and hospitals. I decided to take some insurance classes and take the state insurance exams to get my license in three different states, Arkansas, Mississippi and Tennessee specializing in Health and Life. This way, I would be able to conduct Medicare Seminars for people turning age sixty-five to help educate them so they would be able to make the best healthcare decisions for themselves at the most critical times of their lives, and they would have a clearer understanding of how the Medicare system worked. I saw this as a way to reach out and help other people, which had always been my goal and objective in life. Having knowledge about health insurance offered a large marketing opportunity, simply because of the tremendous influx of Baby Boomers turning age sixty-five. Needless to say, getting my license was an overwhelmingly successful idea. After a few years, I had acquired hundreds of happy customers, and I made a great choice of work with the insurance company that my mother had her insurance with for many years. In my first year with the insurance company, they had an incentive program to recognize their top sales performers in the country. This contest was based on the highest customer sales for the year. There were only six months left in the year when I started, and I was determined to win the trip for two to Ireland, even though all management thought it was impossible. I set my goal and worked toward reaching it by the end of the year. At the end of the year, I had achieved that goal and was one of the company's top sales producers. Therefore, receiving special recognition and winning the fantastic trip to Ireland for two, with senior management, and other winners from around the country. It was a fabulous trip, and one that I will never forget. During my insurance career, I was able to help so many people which was fulfilling and rewarding, and was able to add a lot of income to my retirement savings plan.

Then my brother who lived nearby had a brain seizure, even though he had no history or family history of seizures. Over the next year, I spent time helping his daughters to care for him until he passed, and about four months after my brother's death, my oldest son died from an Asthma attack. All of these recent deaths in the family left me with no immediate family in Arkansas. We had always known that we didn't really want to spend the rest of our retirement years in the south. Therefore, we began to venture out taking what we called road trips in our motorhome to check out other parts of the United States to see if we were interested in retiring there. After many trips across the country, we finally decided that we would move back to California where we would be near our son, daughter and two grandchildren. After making the decision, we sold our home in Arkansas, and had a new home built in a beautiful area in Southern California where we had built what I thought was my "take me to glory home," which was my plan, but God had a different plan, and that was how we ended up living in Arkansas caring for my elderly parents. Now that we have moved back to California, I am hoping that this is our last pack up and relocate. We absolutely love living in the desert, and being closer to our family. As we age, we ask ourselves who will take care of us? At least with us living closer they will not have to worry about traveling across country to visit or help to care for us if ever needed.

Now that we were back in California, I have been trying to relax and enjoy my retirement years. I am a very active person, and I find it hard to just relax and do nothing, but it is my goal to learn to slow down and relax. I spend a lot of time at the clubhouse working out and participating in water aerobic exercise classes, and I have finally decided to really retire. Even though every other year, I take the health insurance exam to renew my insurance license. I have no plans to actively work the business, even though I love being able to help other people, and often find myself helping someone to understand how Medicare works, I find this very fulfilling knowing that I was able to help someone. We keep very busy traveling all over the world seeing new places and learning new things. Life has been good, and we have truly been blessed. I thank God every day for all the blessings that He has given us. I know that I am who I am through the grace of God, and all our blessings have come through Him. I have always lived my life based on belief, confidence, faith and hope. I believe that all things are possible if you just believe, have confidence and faith in God and yourself. It is hope that has allowed me to see the bright side of things, and it has been hope that has given me joy over the years. My favorite saying that I have lived my life by all of these years, is, "Always shoot for the stars, and if you miss, you will land on the moon."

Chapter Eighteen
God's Greatest Gift

One of God's greatest gifts is children. In raising my children, I tried to pass down the family legacy from my great-grandfather regarding the importance of education, and to instill in each of them that they could be and do anything in life they wanted as long as they believed in themselves, and that there is no such word as can't because the future belongs to those who believe in the beauty of their dreams, and the kind of beauty that they should want comes from within, faith, strength, courage, and dignity. I reinforced that they could do anything in life they chose to do when they open their minds to the possibility that they can be successful. I tried to make sure that they understood that their success was in their own hands, and that they were in charge of their own life, and that being successful would offer them an opportunity to shape and control their lives as long as they believed in themselves, and that it was entirely up to them to make it happen if they wanted to create the lifestyle that they want to live. I taught them that success comes to those who act, not to those who remain idle, waiting, wishing and wondering. I reminded them to always resist the human tendency to say that something is impossible even before they examine the possibilities, because if they accept the possibility that they can be successful, they will be successful. I constantly stressed the importance of education, and that it was up to them to keep the family legacy alive and pass it on to their children. I taught them to always remember that their future depends on them, and that they should always be proud of the shoulders that they stand on. Most importantly, they should keep their faith and trust in God. I know that God has been with me in everything that I have done in life.

My primary goal in life was to ensure that my children got a good education even if I had to make some sacrifices. The school system where we lived in Rego Park was very good even though they did not offer that personalized teacher student interaction. In my daughter's sophomore year, she had an opportunity to attend a two-week Summer Leadership Training Program at the New York Military Academy that was located in upstate New York. At the end of the summer training program, she was approached by one of the Majors who shared with her that the Military Academy was going coed, and that they wanted to offer her an opportunity to be one of the first of eight female students to attend the Military Academy. He told her that she was being recruited based on her outgoing personality, academic, music and athletic achievements. She was just going into her junior year in high school. She had enjoyed the environment at the Military Academy during the two-week summer camp, and was excited about the opportunity of going to school there and being one of the first girls to change history at the school. After many discussions with her, I decided that she could go to the academy even though tuition was about $30,000 a year. The New York Military Academy is a college preparatory private boarding school located about sixty miles from New York City. It is one of the oldest military schools in the United States for students in grades eight through twelfth. Originally it was an all-boys' school until they started admitting girls, and my daughter was one of the first of eight girls to attend the academy. The academy's mission is to develop the students' mind, body, and character in order to prepare them for future higher education, and how to be an effective leader and responsible citizen. Every cadet is prepared for college, and it is a great place for students to develop great life habits, honor, and leadership. The school focused on building self-esteem and problem solving. In her senior year, she was the first female cadet to be promoted to Captain which is the highest rank a cadet can hold at the academy. Being Captain was a rank that she truly enjoyed. Every weekend the academy had an outdoor drill parade, and my daughter played the clarinet. Most weekends I would go to the parade, and after the parade, I would take my daughter and some of her friends off campus for lunch. My daughter enjoyed having the opportunity to go to school with students from all over the world, which was an exciting and interesting experience. When she graduated, she was offered a scholarship to attend West Point Military Academy which is one of the best and most prestigious military academies in the world. She turned it down because she did not want to be obligated to serve active duty for four years after graduating. However, it was indeed an honor for her to have been accepted, because they have a 10 percent acceptance rate, and they are very selective. After graduating she received a lot of scholarship offers from many different universities based on her academic, athletic and military achievements. When she finally narrowed it down, she decided to accept the scholarship from the University of Wisconsin in Madison, where she would be in their marching band playing the clarinet, and on their women's track team. In her first year, she signed up for the Reserve Officers Training Corps (ROTC) program and was commissioned to Second Lieutenant. At that time, we were living in New York, but she wanted to go to the University of Wisconsin, because she was born in Wisconsin, and I grew up there, and had attended the University of Wisconsin. "Daughter like mother."

In her junior year at Wisconsin, she wanted to transfer to Central State University which is a Historically Black College located in Wilberforce, Ohio. She wanted to go where there were more Black students, because she felt that she was losing her Black identity. In choosing a place to live, I would choose a place that I felt was safe, and had the best school system in order to allow my children to get a good education, which meant that all the grade schools and high schools that she had attended had none or very few Black students. Reluctantly, I agreed to her transferring to Central State University where she played in the band, and was a cheerleader. Two years later, she graduated with a degree in Business Administration. She received many job offers from large corporations for sales and marketing positions. Her resume stood out because of her academic, athletic and military academy achievements and experience. In her senior year, I spent time helping her to prepare for job interview i.e., how to write a resume, what questions to ask, and how to answer questions, eye contact, and of course how to dress and sit during the interview session. She ended up accepting a position with a pharmaceutical company in sales. While working, she decided to sign up and serve in the Army Reserves one weekend a month, and two weeks per year learning how to keep her skills sharp. She started in the Army Reserves as a Second Lieutenant, and was promoted to First Lieutenant, and then to Captain. I am so proud of her, and all of her accomplishments in life, and the transfer to Central State University was the greatest thing that could have happened for her. I know that the world is my oyster and she is my shiniest pearl! She has two beautiful children that she has passed down the family legacy from her great-great-grandfather about the importance of education, and both of her children graduated from Historically Black Colleges.

My daughter's son graduated from Grambling State University in Grambling, Louisiana where he played football, and her daughter from Bennett College which is a private four-year historically black liberal arts college for women, and is located in

Greensboro, North Carolina. They are both working and have successful business careers.

My son had an opportunity to attend Rumsey Hall School which is an independent, coed junior boarding and day school for students in kindergarten through ninth grade, and is ranked as one of the top prep schools in the country. They have an enrollment of about 300 students from all over the world and tuition is currently $68,000 a year. The campus is located on 231 beautiful acres along the scenic Bantam River in Connecticut. Each dorm is supervised by dorm parents who live in the dorms and treat the students like their own family. The school focuses on teaching each student how to develop and assess their individual standpoint, and they strive to expand the power of each child's inner voice through social-emotional learning programs, and overall school culture, which gives each student a chance to surpass their personal limits, and one of their primary focuses is public speaking which is an essential function of Rumsey Hall's education. Their students matriculate to remarkable secondary schools. The activities that they offered are basketball, volleyball, soccer, hockey, skating, and mountain biking. My son played hockey. On weekends the students had a large selection of activities to choose from, i.e., movies, skiing, hiking, camping and many other weekend activities. The school was close to where we lived and I spent a lot of weekends on campus enjoying the student parent weekend activities. After finishing up at Rumsey Hall, he went to Montclair High School in New Jersey where he excelled as a student and athlete. He was an outstanding football player, and played the position of free safety, and helped the school to win many games. He was on the school's track team, and ran the anchor leg for the nation's No.1 ranked high school mile relay team, where he excelled and received many awards. After graduating from high school, he was recruited by many universities but decided to go to Notre Dame where Lou Holtz was the coach of the Notre Dame Fighting Irish football team in South Bend, Indiana. For four years he played cornerback for

Notre Dame at the Notre Dame stadium which had a capacity of 77,622 fans, and we had an opportunity to go to many of his home games. This is a published quote from Lou Holtz regarding my son, "He is one of the most gifted athletes on the team, he has tremendous speed, and he has intelligence and natural leadership." After graduating from Notre Dame University with a degree in Finance, he was drafted by the Cincinnati Bengals. After playing professional football, and spending twenty-six remarkable years as an entrepreneur in the health and fitness business, where he was able to use his sales and marketing skills. After closing that business, he decided to use his financial background skills, and has a successful business working with business owners, executives, and nonprofit organizations on innovative retirement strategies that will allow them to have financial resources to sustain their vision for decades, and leave a legacy. He is fully devoted to whatever he sets out to do, and is definitely a workaholic and a real mama's boy. I always told him that he was my "Sunshine" because he knows how to light up my day.

My oldest son, that my parents raised, decided after graduating from high school that he did not want to go to college. He had always been passionate about cars, so he wanted to go to a certified automotive mechanic trade school to gain the technical skills and hands-on experience needed to work in an auto mechanic shop, and where he could work for my brother in his automotive repair shop, helping to keep cars, trucks, and other vehicles running safely and efficiently. This is a job that he loved, and he truly enjoyed working with my brother and his uncle.

I have always been willing to make sacrifices to ensure that my children received a good education. However, there were three things that I was not willing to sacrifice: my family, my heart, or my dignity. I know that raising children is not an easy job. Therefore, I focused on three things, teaching, preaching and praying. Teaching my children right from wrong while they were young, and as they became teenagers, I did a lot of preaching to reinforce the teaching, and once they became young adults, I did a lot of praying. This is a special message for each of my children and grandchildren. "Never forget that I love you, and I hope that you will always believe in yourself as much as I believe in you, and if life knocks you down, know that I will always be there for you. I can't promise you that I will be there for the rest of your life, but I can promise to love you for the rest of my life."

FAMILY PICTURE

SON

DAUGHTER

SON

ME AND SPOUSE

GRANDAUGHTER

GRANDSON

◇

Chapter Nineteen
Facing the Greatest Battle of My Life

During my lifetime, I have always been a warrior fighting many battles and wars in order to overcome many obstacles and roadblocks that I had to face in life. However, the battle that I now face will definitely be the hardest battle that I have to fight. During the past thirty-five years, I had a mammogram every year to ensure that there were no signs of breast cancer. The annual mammograms always came back negative. Last year, my doctor ordered a CT scan for another health issue. The test results showed a suspicious nodule in my left breast which was missed by the annual mammogram, and could not be felt by doing a self-breast exam. My oncologist set up an appointment for a biopsy of the nodule in the left breast, and the test results confirmed malignancy in the left breast duct. After meetings with all the doctors, we decided that the lumpectomy surgery would be the best for me. During the surgery, the surgeon removed the small nodule in the left breast, and two lymph nodes under my left arm to ensure that the cancer had not spread to other areas of the body.

The test results from the surgery did not show any signs that the cancer had spread into other areas of the breast, or into the lymph nodes. Therefore, I did not need additional surgery or Chemotherapy. However. I would need to have four weeks of radiation treatments to the left breast area to ensure that there were no other cancer cells. I am currently on a six months follow-up program to have a Diagnostic mammogram, and a CT scan to ensure that there are no cancer cells in the breast or have spread to other parts of the body. Needless to say, it was a roller coaster year, with a lot of doctor appointments during the height of the COVID crisis.

When you hear that you have cancer, it's hard to remove that word from your mind, and most people fear the worst. During my first six months, it was extremely difficult to not stress out daily, I had to constantly remind myself that the final outcome of this challenge was in God's hands. I just tried to focus on keeping my faith and praying a lot, with the support of my husband, my children, grandchildren, family, and all my awesome caring, praying friends that were there to help keep me strong, when there were days that I was not sure if I would be strong enough to get through this. I would like to extend a special thanks to my family, and especially my good friends who are like stars, I don't always see them, but I know that they are there. It was my faith that got me through this problem, and that has given me the ability to know how to handle it. I know that having faith does not always take you out of the problem that you face, but it can take you through it. It has been my faith that has given me the ability to be able to handle what I am going through today. I pray each day that I will have comfort, strength, courage, and find healing and peace while dealing with breast cancer.

Chapter Twenty
Family Memories/It's Now Up to You/
The Best Day of My Life

Family memories are like strands of thread that have been woven together to create the fabric of life that tells the story of my life, and my family's journey over the past 162 years. In order for my family to have survived all these years, each family member had to have stamina, grit and determination to succeed in life, while reinforcing faith, and hope, and always believing that tomorrow was going to be better, even though today had been great. Each generation must continue to remember that their parents, and grandparents passed their dreams to them, and it's now up to them, to keep the dream alive, and pass it on to their children regarding the importance of education, and believing that all things are possible if they have faith, hope, and believe that better days are coming, by keeping their eyes on the tunnel. I am very proud of what I have achieved in my life simply by believing in myself, and that all things are possible, and there is no word as "can't" if you believe in yourself...because if you think you can...you can, and if you think you can't, you are right you can't. I have always believed that I could overcome any obstacles to achieve my goals simply by just "imagining myself successful," because it is success that breeds self-confidence.

I have attempted throughout my memoir to be impeccably realistic about the challenges, frustrations, obstacles, and roadblocks that I had to face and overcome in my personal life, and in the corporate world. I have shared with you the pitfalls, pressures, politics and prejudices that I had to encounter especially while living in the south. I shared with you my experience of being a mother at age fourteen. I've told you about the sacrifices that I had to make in order to have lived the life that I have. Now I want to give women one last thing—encouragement. Encouragement about the future of businesswomen, and encouragement about your own future. Remember that ambition is no longer a dirty word. The women's movement has made you and your desires to seek wealth and power socially acceptable. Even today a position in sales and marketing is an idea springboard to other executive positions within a company. Know that you do affect others either for good or for bad, positively or negatively, and that's why it is important to maintain a proper perspective, and a good attitude because your actions and deeds can have an effect on other people. You should learn from your mistakes, and then forget them, don't allow a few errors in judgement to erode your self-confidence. There are a lot of things in my life that I was the first woman, or first Black woman, but what is important today is that I was not the last woman. People often ask me if I have any regrets about the decisions that I have made in life. The answer is Yes, I had a few regrets, but too few to even mention. I did what I had to do, and I saw it through without exceptions. I have learned over the years to count my blessings and not my problems. I am often reminded of what my dad would always tell me, "Never let the things you want, make you forget the things you have." Sometimes, I feel like I have been on a journey most of my life, but now I feel that I have reached my destination, and

I am finally ready to settle down and enjoy my "Golden Years."

Today when I awoke, I suddenly realized that this is the best day of my life. There were times when I wondered if I would make it to today; but I did, and I am going to celebrate what an unbelievable life I have had so far: the accomplishments, the many blessings, and, yes, even the hardships because they served to make me stronger. I will go through this day with my head held high, and with a happy heart. Today, I will share my excitement for life with someone else. I will go out of my way to make someone smile. I will tell someone I love just how deeply I care for them and how much they mean to me. Today is the day that I will quit worrying about what I don't have and start being thankful for all the wonderful things God has already given me. I'll remember that to worry is just a waste of time because my faith in God and His Divine Plan assures me that everything will be fine. As the day ends, I will lay my head down on my pillow, and I will thank God for the best day of my life. I will sleep with contentment, excitement and expectations because I know that tomorrow is going to be the best day of my life. Sometimes, when I look back over my life at all the challenges, obstacles, and roadblocks that I had to overcome, and still face today, I just look up, smile and say, "I know that was you, God. Thanks!"

REFLECTIONS – "Looking in the mirror, when you look in the mirror how others see you is not important. What is important is how you see yourself, that's what means everything in life."